Healing the Broken Heart

Navigating Grief and Loss After the Death of a Child

By
Dee Walters

This book is written:

Dedicated to my Amazing Son
Dray Robert Clark Walters A.K.A. Superman

Introduction

Every second in life is a miracle, a gift to be treasured. And every second in a life shared with a child is a marvel beyond words. It is an unending cycle of laughter, tears, hopes, fears, joyous milestones, and heart-wrenching moments. But what happens when a second becomes an eternity when a heartbeat silences and time seems to stand still? What happens when a parent is forced to face the unimaginable - the death of a child?

For those who have never experienced such a loss, it is a horror too profound to comprehend. For those who have, it is a reality too painful to bear. It is a journey through darkness that no parent should ever have to embark on, yet many do. This is the journey that I, too, was forced to undertake.

On an ordinary day, a day filled with promise and light, my world was shattered. My son, my beautiful boy on the cusp of his 21st birthday, was suddenly taken from us. His laughter, spirit, and dreams were all extinguished in the blink of an eye. The hospital, the life support machines, and the hopeless prognosis are all etched into my memory, a haunting echo of a nightmare that refuses to end. And then, the silence was so deafening that it drowned out the rest of the world.

In the blink of an eye, my world was irrevocably changed. I was plunged into disbelief, despair, and indescribable pain. I was forced to navigate a labyrinth of grief, each twist and turn more torturous than the last. I faced the unbearable task of saying goodbye to my child and accepting that I would never again hear his voice, see his smile, or hold him in my arms.

But amidst the grief and the pain, there was also love. A love that transcended the boundaries of life and death and held the power to heal, comfort, and inspire. And it is this love, this unbreakable bond between a parent and a child, that I wish to share with you.

As a parent grieving the loss of a child, you are confronted with pain so consuming that it can feel like you are being swallowed by it. It's a loss so unnatural and devastating that it defies the natural order of life. Parents are supposed to see their children grow, flourish, and eventually forge their paths in life. Losing a child is like having a piece of your heart torn away, leaving a void that seems impossible to fill.

You might find yourself wrestling with emotions that threaten to overwhelm you. The immense sadness that engulfs you may be accompanied by feelings of anger, guilt, and even denial. You may ask, "Why my child?" or "What could I have done differently?" It's natural to look for reasons and answers, but often, there are none to be found.

Your days may seem colorless, your nights filled with restless thoughts and haunting dreams. Once familiar routines and places may serve as stark reminders of your loss, turning the ordinary into the extraordinarily painful. You might feel detached, like navigating through life in a fog, feeling disconnected from those around you, even those closest to you.

The world may seem to move on, but time might feel frozen for you. You might feel pressure to "get over" your loss and "move on" with your life. But grief doesn't work on a timetable, and it's not something you simply get over, it's a journey, a unique process for each individual.

The pain of losing a child can also strain your relationships. Others might struggle to understand your grief or to know how to support you. You may feel isolated, even in a crowd, as if alone in your suffering.

You may find yourself grappling with existential questions about life, death, and the fairness of it all. Your faith may be tested, or you may find solace in it. You may question your identity, purpose, and life's meaning.

I understand these feelings because I've lived them. I've felt the soul-crushing pain of losing a child and the emotions that follow. I've faced the darkness and walked through it, step by painful step. I understand your struggle, pain, and heartache because it's a journey I've taken myself.

Grief is not a stranger to any of us. We have all lost someone or something at some point. But the death of a child is an experience that rips apart the fabric of what we believe life to be. It is a cataclysmic event that does not abide by the natural order of things. Parents are not meant to bury their children. Yet, here I was, plunged into an unimaginable abyss of sorrow.

This book is not a roadmap through the wilderness of grief. Each journey is personal, unique, and deeply intimate. No one-size-fits-all guidebook can navigate you through the rough terrain of this devastating loss. But I hope that by sharing my story and chronicling the raw, unvarnished truth of my grief, I can reach out to you in your darkest moments. I hope to tell you that while you may feel utterly alone, you are not.

I have learned that grief is not a mountain to be conquered but a river to be navigated. It changes course, ebbs and flows, rages and calms. There are rapids, waterfalls, and calm pools where you can catch your breath. But the river keeps flowing, and so must we.

In this book, you will find my story— a tapestry of love, loss, and a painstaking journey toward healing. It's woven with threads of despair and hope, pain and resilience, tears and occasional smiles. But most importantly, it is a story of survival because even when faced with the most profound loss, we find a way to keep going.

I invite you to join me on this journey, not as a spectator but as a companion. We may walk in the shadows of grief, but we do not walk alone. Through my words, I hope you find solace, understanding, and perhaps even the strength to face another day. Because as impossible as it may seem, the sun still rises, even after the darkest night.

Welcome to our shared journey through the valleys of grief towards the hope of a new dawn.

Chapter 1: Understanding Grief

Grief is a chameleon, always changing its hue. It has a thousand faces and a thousand ways of expressing itself. Yet, in all its forms, it is universally recognized as an extreme response to loss. When my son's life ended so abruptly, grief swept in like a torrential downpour, without giving me a moment to grab an umbrella or find shelter.

I remember feeling this dreadful, suffocating weight on my chest. It was as if I was trying to breathe underwater. Suddenly, I was navigating a world that had turned colorless, the vibrancy of life drained away. And in this new, harsh reality, I found myself grappling with the pervasive, multifaceted nature of grief. It was in these early days of pain and confusion that I first encountered the concept of grief's stages, the individuality of the grieving process, and the necessity of acknowledging and validating my sorrow.

Grief is not a linear journey, nor a fixed period after which you suddenly emerge healed. It's a complex maze of emotions, and understanding this maze is the first step towards finding your way through it. In this chapter, we delve deeper into these aspects, shedding light on the intricate process of grieving, in hopes of helping you navigate your own path through the pain.

Hold my hand, dear reader. Let's embark on this journey together, and through understanding, perhaps we will find a semblance of solace.

The Stages of Grief

The loss of my child threw me headfirst into a whirlwind of emotions, a storm I had never before encountered. I found myself floundering, consumed by an abyss of emotions I didn't recognize. It wasn't until I stumbled upon the work of Elisabeth Kübler-Ross, a Swiss-American psychiatrist, that I began to make some sense of the emotional tempest I was enduring. Kübler-Ross proposed a model that outlines five stages of grief. They are denial, anger, bargaining, depression, and acceptance. It's crucial to remember, though, that not everyone experiences these stages in the same order, or even experiences them all. Here's how I encountered them:

1. Denial: The stage of denial is as paralyzing as it is perplexing. It was the world's cruelest paradox: the sun rose and set as it always had, people went about their day, laughing, working, living, and yet my world had come to an excruciating halt. My son, the boy with the infectious laughter and bright dreams, was gone. Just gone. It was unfathomable, a concept too horrifying to absorb.

Denial, in this haze of grief, served as a temporary, yet necessary, reprieve. It cloaked the harshness of reality, numbing the sting of the loss. I felt like a marionette, moving through the motions of life without truly living it. There were moments when I would reach out to call him for dinner, only to be met by an echoing silence. Other times, I'd expect to see his name light up on my phone, his voice ready to greet me on the other end. But those calls never came.

This disorienting denial was not a conscious refusal to acknowledge the truth. It was a primal reaction, a protective shield woven by my mind to cushion the sudden blow. It was as if my psyche had wrapped itself in a cocoon, seeking refuge from a reality too agonizing to accept. It was a limbo, a strange twilight zone between the life I had known and the life I was forced to face.

There were quiet nights when denial would wane, and the brutal truth would seep into my consciousness. Those moments were incredibly painful, like sharp, frigid gusts of wind slicing through my soul. But each time, the veil of denial would descend again, offering me a respite from the gnawing pain, a chance to gather my strength for the long journey of grief that was yet to come.

In the dance of grief, denial leads first, setting a slow, disorienting tempo. But it's not a permanent state. With time, it recedes, allowing us to confront our loss and the myriad emotions that come with it. Its purpose, as I came to realize, is not to deceive us, but to help us survive the unbearable, until we are ready to endure it.

2. Anger: As the cloak of denial began to thin, anger took its place, fierce and demanding. It was as if a dam broke within me, flooding me with a torrent of fury. I felt anger towards everything — the universe for being so cruel, fate for dealing such a ruthless hand, and myself for not being able to protect my son.

The anger felt like a wildfire, consuming everything in its path. It was a sharp contrast to the numbing disbelief of denial, raw and fervent. I would catch myself clenching my fists until my nails bit into my palms, the physical pain a mirror to the inner turmoil I was grappling with.

"Why him?" I would cry out in the empty silence of my room, my voice ricocheting off the walls. "Why us?" This stage was marked by countless sleepless nights, long hours spent staring at the ceiling, rage boiling within me like a tempest.

And then there was the guilt. It arrived hand in hand with the anger, a nefarious duo that fed off each other. I tormented myself with thoughts of what I could have done differently. Had I missed something? Could I have saved him? It was an endless cycle of self-flagellation that only fueled my rage further.

I had always considered myself a peaceful person, but the anger stage of grief brought out a side of me I barely recognized. It felt uncontrollable, like a wild beast roaring within me. It was daunting, at times even scary, to witness this transition, but I later understood it was a natural, even necessary, part of the grieving process.

Anger, in its own twisted way, is a testament to the depth of our love. It's the heart's revolt against the unacceptable, the unbearable loss of a loved one. It's a step, however agonizing, towards acknowledging the reality of the loss, a step away from the numbing denial. It may be difficult to endure, but it's a sign of progress, a sign of moving through the shadowed valley of grief.

3. Bargaining: After the surge of anger subsided, came a quieter, yet persistent stage - bargaining. A stage characterized by "if onlys" and "what ifs", where the mind attempts to negotiate its way out of the pain.

In my grief, I found myself turning to these hypothetical scenarios. "If only I had insisted on that extra health check-up." "What if I had been there with him that day?" My mind was an incessant loom, weaving a tapestry of alternate realities where my son still lived, laughing, breathing, existing.

Bargaining was my plea to the universe, a desperate bid to rewind time and alter the course of events. I sought solace in a fantasy where I could have done something, anything, to save my child. It was an insidious form of torment, keeping me stuck in a loop of guilt and regret.

But it was not just about the past. It extended to the future too. I found myself making promises, attempting to strike a deal with some higher power. "I'll dedicate my life to charity if I could just wake up from this nightmare," I would whisper into the silence of the night, my words dissolving into a sea of unshed tears.

In hindsight, I realize that bargaining was my mind's attempt at regaining control, trying to make sense of a situation that defied reason. It was an emotional balm, alleviating the harsh sting of reality, if only momentarily.

This stage, while painful, signaled a shift. It was a subtle acknowledgement of the fact that my son was gone, a fact I had skirted around in my denial and anger. Bargaining, in all its desperation, was an indication of the slow, reluctant acceptance of loss, a precursor to the stages to come.

4. Depression: As bargaining began to fade, it made way for a deep and heavy sorrow. This was the stage of depression. Unlike the word 'depression' often used to denote a clinical condition, in the context of the grief stages, it refers to a deep sadness, a feeling of despair that permeates every aspect of your being.

In this stage, the reality of my son's absence felt more pronounced, more final. The world around me lost its color, becoming a grayscale version of what it once was. I found myself engulfed in a pervasive sadness; a sense of despair that made even the simplest tasks feel Herculean.

Every corner of our home echoed with his absence, each item bearing his fingerprints seemed to whisper stories of a life that was no more. His laughter, his dreams, his quirks — everything that made my son who he was — felt like they were slipping away, drowning in an ocean of sorrow I was barely treading.

I withdrew into a shell, distancing myself from the outside world. I would sit for hours, staring blankly out the window, or the pictures of him on the wall, as silent tears trickled down my face. I felt empty, a hollow shell of the person I once was. I grappled with questions that had no answers — Why should I go on? How can I possibly live in a world without my child?

Depression is a stage where grief stops being an abstract concept and becomes a physical reality. It's when you feel the loss in your bones, in every breath you take, in every beat of your heart. It's painful, it's overwhelming, but it's also a testament to the depth of your love, an ode to the bond that you shared with your child.

In its raw, unfiltered form, depression is an acknowledgment of the magnitude of the loss. It's a dark tunnel, but like all tunnels, it has an end. You will emerge, though changed, with a newfound resilience and a greater appreciation for the love and memories you carry.

5. Acceptance: After navigating the tumultuous seas of denial, anger, bargaining, and depression, I stumbled upon the shores of acceptance. Acceptance, contrary to what I initially believed, was not about being 'okay' with my son's death. That was something I knew I could never be. Instead, it was about acknowledging the reality of my loss and learning to live with it.

In this stage, I began to find a new rhythm to my life, a life that would forever carry the imprint of my son's absence. I allowed myself to experience joy without feeling guilty, to remember my son without being consumed by grief. I gave myself permission to continue living, even while a part of me mourned.

Acceptance was not a linear progression from pain to healing; it was a complex dance of two steps forward, one step back. Some days, the pain would resurface, raw and overwhelming, and I'd find myself traversing through the previous stages all over again. But each time, I emerged a little stronger, a little more resilient.

Acceptance was about allowing the memories of my son to coexist with my present and my future. It was about cherishing the love we shared, while opening my heart to new experiences, new joys. Acceptance didn't mean the pain was gone; it meant that I had found a way to hold it, to carry it with grace.

This stage was a testament to human resilience, to our innate capacity to heal and adapt. It was a journey of self-discovery, a journey that required patience, compassion, and an indomitable spirit. In accepting my loss, I discovered a strength I never knew I possessed, a love that transcended death, and a bond that would forever link me to my son.

As you embark on your grief journey, remember that these stages are not rigid compartments you must move through sequentially. They are fluid, overlapping, and revisiting each other in no predictable order. You might not experience all the stages, or you might experience them differently. And that's okay. Grief is as unique as the love we hold for the person we've lost. The important thing is to allow yourself to feel, to grieve, and to heal in your own time, in your own way.

Grief as a Unique and Individual Experience

Grief is not a one-size-fits-all kind of experience. It is as individual as a fingerprint, as unique as the person experiencing it. Just as the relationship we had with the person we've lost was singular and special, so too is our response to their loss. There is no definitive roadmap, no universally applicable guide to grieving. Your grief will be as unique as your love for your child was, and still is.

I recall the countless times people attempted to console me with phrases like "I understand how you feel" or "it gets better with time." Though well-intentioned, these statements felt hollow, somehow missing the depth of my pain. They couldn't possibly understand the nuances of my grief, the specific shape and weight of my loss.

At times, I felt a pang of guilt for not grieving 'right', for not fitting into the stages of grief as neatly as I thought I should. My grief was chaotic, it ebbed and flowed with no predictable pattern. It would sneak up on me in the middle of a mundane task or a quiet moment, and suddenly, I would be hit by a tidal wave of sorrow.

There were also moments when my grief seemed to morph into something softer, something that allowed me to experience joy or laughter without being ensnared by guilt. There were instances when I would find comfort in unexpected places, in memories of my son, in the stories we shared, or even in dreams where he still lived and breathed.

This journey taught me that there is no 'right' or 'wrong' way to grieve. It's a deeply personal process, shaped by a myriad of factors—our relationship with the deceased, our coping mechanisms, our support system, our belief system, and even our past experiences with loss.

While the stages of grief provide a useful framework, they are not an exhaustive or definitive map of the grief experience. They are, at best, signposts in an unfamiliar terrain, shedding light on some possible reactions to loss.

Grief, in all its complexity, is a testament to our capacity to love. It's an intimate journey, one that eventually leads us to a place of understanding and reconciliation. A place where we can cherish our loved one's memory, honor our grief, and still find a way to move forward with life.

Remember, as you traverse this journey, to be kind to yourself. Respect your individual process and timeline. Do not rush to 'get over' your loss, for grief is not a barrier to be overcome but a testament to a love that was, and still is, deep.

Acknowledging and Validating Your Pain

Grief, in its raw and relentless form, often feels like an immense, incomprehensible abyss. It's a kind of pain that hits at the very core of our being. We wish we could run from it, but there is no escape. It's a storm that we must weather. But in weathering this storm, acknowledging, and validating our pain becomes the first step towards healing.

When my son passed away, the world seemed to collapse around me. Everything lost its color, its vibrancy. It was like a dark cloud had descended, shrouding me in an unending night. My heart felt heavy, as though a stone had been lodged there. And I remember the tears, oh the tears, that came in torrents, like a river breaking its banks. My sorrow was a tangible, visceral thing, an entity all of its own.

At first, I attempted to hide my grief, to wear the mask of 'normalcy' that society often expects from us. I buried my pain under the pretense of being strong—for my family, for my surviving children, for the world. But this only served to intensify my suffering. Grief, when ignored, only grows in strength and scope.

Then came the realization—a painful yet necessary one—that I had to confront my grief, to meet it face to face. I had to give my pain the space to exist, to breathe. I had to validate it, to acknowledge its legitimacy, its right to be there. For this pain was a testament to my love for my child, a love that transcended even death.

Grief, I came to understand, was not something to be 'managed' or 'fixed'. It's not a condition but a natural response to loss. It's okay to feel overwhelmed by it, to be engulfed by its intensity. It's okay to cry, to scream, to sit in silence. It's okay to not be okay.

It's also important to remember that your grief might take a different shape or form than that of others. Some people might cry openly, while others might grieve in silence. Some might find comfort in talking about their lost loved ones, while others might prefer to keep their thoughts private. All of these reactions, and more, are normal. They are your body, your heart, your soul's way of processing loss.

Acknowledging and validating our pain also requires us to be honest about our emotions. We tend to hide from feelings that make us uncomfortable or that we fear might be judged by others. But in the wake of such a loss, you might experience a myriad of emotions. There could be guilt, anger, disbelief, despair, fear, or even relief, and these emotions could shift rapidly, like a tempestuous sea.

Take guilt, for example. I remember feeling an intense sense of guilt after my son's death. I kept replaying the day he died over and over in my mind. If only I had heard the phone ringing. If only I had been there. If only... This guilt clung to me, a constant companion in my grief.

However, guilt, like any other emotion, doesn't arise in a vacuum. It was borne from my deep love for my son and the desperate wish that things had been different. When I began to view my guilt in this light, it became less of a tormentor and more of a testament to the depth of my love.

Being open about these emotions, acknowledging them, can help dissipate their overwhelming power. It's a hard process, but it's essential for healing. Consider seeking a safe space where you can express these feelings openly. This could be with a trusted friend or family member, a support group, or a mental health professional.

During this time, it's also crucial to remember to take care of your physical health. Grief can be incredibly draining, both emotionally and physically. It's common to experience changes in sleep patterns, appetite, and energy levels. Try to maintain a regular routine, eat healthy meals, and get enough rest.

At the same time, don't forget to give yourself permission to experience moments of respite. Brief periods where the weight of grief lightens doesn't mean you love or miss your child any less. It's okay to smile or laugh. It's okay to enjoy a beautiful sunset or the company of a good friend. These moments don't betray your grief; they are merely acknowledgments of life's complexity, where joy and sorrow can coexist.

The journey through grief is undeniably challenging, and at times you may feel lost and alone. But remember, by acknowledging your pain and validating your emotions, you're taking crucial steps towards healing. You're affirming that it's okay to grieve, to hurt, and eventually, it's okay to heal. By acknowledging your pain, you're not leaving your lost child behind, but carrying their memory forward into a future where love endures, even in the face of loss.

Chapter 2: Coping with Loss

As the dust of the initial shock settles, the reality of loss seeps in, and we find ourselves on a long, winding road that signifies the journey of grief. This path is unlike any other, marked with unique milestones and obstacles that challenge our resilience. As we embark on this journey, we must keep in mind that the objective isn't about getting back to the 'old normal,' but about finding ways to cope, to adapt, and to continue living meaningfully in the absence of our loved one.

In this chapter, we will explore the avenues of self-care that play a critical role in coping with loss. We will examine emotional self-care, recognizing our emotional needs and navigating the tumultuous sea of emotions. We will touch upon physical self-care, understanding how grief affects our body and how essential it is to maintain physical wellness as we grieve.

Lastly, we will delve into spiritual and cultural perspectives on grief and loss. We will explore how these perspectives can provide comfort, meaning, and a sense of connection amidst our grief.

Each person's journey through grief is unique, and in these unique experiences, we might find universal truths that bind us all, offering solace and hope in our darkest hours. This journey won't be easy, but remember, you are not alone. With each step, each stumble, and each triumph, we move forward, carrying with us the indelible memory of our child, a testament of enduring love and strength.

Emotional Self-Care in the Face of Grief

In the aftermath of losing a child, the tempest of emotions that you find yourself in can be overwhelming, sometimes paralyzing. During these times, it's vital to remember that self-care is not a luxury, but a necessity. Engaging in emotional self-care means giving yourself the permission to feel, to mourn, and to heal at your own pace. This section aims to provide some guidance on navigating your emotional landscape while ensuring your emotional well-being.

a. Recognize Your Emotions: The first step towards emotional self-care is acknowledging your feelings, no matter how difficult or uncomfortable they might be. There may be days filled with intense sadness, moments of anger, or times of guilt and regret. All these emotions are an integral part of your journey through grief. They are signposts on the road, markers of your progress, rather than impediments. Recognizing them is not a sign of weakness; instead, it is a testament to your strength and resilience. Be gentle with yourself; there's no need to rush or force these emotions away.

b. Express Your Feelings: Bottling up emotions can lead to emotional exhaustion. Find safe and healthy outlets to express what you're feeling. This could be through writing in a journal, painting, or even talking to a trusted friend, family member, or grief counselor. These outlets can provide a release for pent-up emotions, making them more manageable over time.

c. Reach Out for Support: As you walk this path, remember you do not have to walk it alone. Reach out to people around you for support. Be honest about how you're feeling and what you need. If you feel more comfortable speaking to someone who has undergone a similar experience, consider joining a support group for parents who have lost a child. These groups can provide a safe space for you to express your emotions without fear of judgment.

d. Practice Mindfulness: Grief can often feel like a whirlwind that sweeps us off our feet. Practicing mindfulness can provide an anchor in these turbulent times. This involves focusing on the present moment without judgment. It could be as simple as taking a few moments each day to focus on your breathing or spending time in nature. By grounding yourself in the present, you can reduce feelings of anxiety and overwhelm.

e. Therapy and Counseling: Seeking professional help can be incredibly beneficial in navigating your grief. A therapist or counselor can provide you with the tools and strategies to manage your emotions and work through your grief in a healthy and productive way.

Emotional self-care is not a one-size-fits-all approach. What works for one person may not work for another. The most important thing is to find what works best for you and to remember that it's okay to prioritize your emotional well-being. Your feelings matter, your experiences matter, and most importantly, you matter. Your grief is your own, and in acknowledging and respecting that, you honor not only your feelings but also the memory of your child.

At the end of the day, emotional self-care is about compassion, for your child, for your family, but most importantly, for yourself. Because you, too, are deserving of care, love, and healing. Remember, it's okay to not be okay, and it's okay to take the time and space you need to heal.

Physical Self-Care and Grief

In the tide of grief, amid the emotional turmoil, the physical aspect of self-care can often be overlooked. However, taking care of your body plays an instrumental role in your overall well-being and capacity to process grief. In this section, we'll explore some ways to incorporate physical self-care into your journey of healing.

a. Nutrition: During times of intense emotional distress, eating habits can often be disrupted. You may find yourself not eating enough, eating too much, or not consuming a balanced diet. Make a conscious effort to nourish your body with balanced meals. Eating foods rich in vitamins and minerals can not only keep your body functioning optimally but can also positively affect your mood and energy levels.

b. Exercise: Physical activity might be the last thing on your mind while grieving, but even a small amount can help. Exercise releases endorphins, the body's natural mood lifters, and can help reduce feelings of depression and anxiety. You don't have to engage in strenuous workouts – a gentle walk, some light stretching, or yoga can be beneficial.

c. Rest: Grief can be exhausting, both emotionally and physically. Prioritize rest and ensure you're getting adequate sleep. If you're having difficulty sleeping, consider creating a calming bedtime routine or seek professional help if needed.

d. Medical Care: Don't neglect regular check-ups or ignore any physical symptoms you may be experiencing. Grief can manifest physically and it's important to communicate with your healthcare provider about any changes you've noticed since your loss.

e. Mind-Body Connection: Practices like meditation, yoga, and deep-breathing exercises can help you feel more connected to your body, reduce stress, and promote emotional balance. They offer a quiet space for reflection and can be a comforting routine during chaotic times.

While these strategies may seem small, they can make a substantial difference in your physical health and your ability to navigate your grief. However, remember that it's okay to have days where these tasks feel overwhelming. Just like your emotional journey, your physical self-care journey is personal and individual. Listen to your body, give it the care it needs, and most importantly, be gentle with yourself.

This process is not about striving for perfection. It's about doing the best you can, one day at a time. In taking care of your physical health, you are honoring your journey of healing, and you are affirming that you, as much as anyone in the universe, deserve care and compassion.

Spiritual and Cultural Perspectives on Grief and Loss

Spirituality and cultural beliefs can be a source of solace during grief, a lighthouse amidst the storm, guiding you back to your path when the sorrow feels like an endless sea. In this part of our journey, we will explore the varied spiritual and cultural perspectives on grief and loss, and how they might provide comfort and understanding.

a. Spiritual Beliefs and Practices: For many, faith or spiritual beliefs offer a broader perspective to understand and make sense of the loss. Prayer, meditation, reading religious texts, or engaging in spiritual rituals can provide a sense of peace and acceptance. These practices can create a safe space for expressing emotions and seeking comfort. Moreover, they can also reinforce a sense of connection with the lost loved one, providing solace in the belief of an afterlife or rebirth.

b. Cultural Rituals and Traditions: Different cultures have unique traditions and rituals around death and mourning. These can range from specific burial rites, periods of mourning, commemorative events, or annual remembrances.

Engaging in these traditions can help one feel connected to their community, and the collective acknowledgment of grief can be a powerful force of comfort and healing.

c. Community and Shared Grief: Within your cultural or spiritual community, shared grief can be a collective journey of healing. Being part of a group where your loss is recognized, and your grief is shared can help lessen feelings of isolation. It's in these spaces where stories are shared, memories are honored, and the deceased are celebrated, ensuring their enduring presence in our hearts.

d. Seeking Guidance: Spiritual leaders, mentors, or elders can be invaluable sources of comfort and guidance. Their wisdom, coupled with their understanding of your spiritual and cultural background, can provide a uniquely empathetic perspective. They can help you navigate your grief within the framework of your beliefs and values.

e. Nature and Grief: Many spiritual and cultural perspectives see a deep connection between us and the natural world. In times of loss, turning to nature can be therapeutic. The cycles of nature — the seasons changing, the rise and fall of the sun, the ebb and flow of the tide — can serve as reminders of life's impermanence and the ongoing cycle of life and death.

Amid sorrow, turning to your spiritual roots or cultural practices can be a beacon of hope. However, it's essential to remember that there is no 'right' or 'wrong' way to grieve within your belief system. These tools and practices are there to support you, to offer comfort, and to guide you toward healing in a way that resonates with your personal beliefs and values. Ultimately, your spiritual or cultural path through grief is as unique as you are, and it's essential to honor that journey in your own way.

Chapter 3: Navigating Relationships After Loss

The heartache of losing a child leaves a seismic fracture within the family unit, creating waves that radiate outwards, touching every relationship you hold dear. Suddenly, you find yourself lost in a labyrinth of unspoken pain, enduring silent meals and sleepless nights. The sense of unity that once existed is replaced by a heavy silence, punctuated only by the echoes of your child's laughter now lingering as a haunting memory. This chapter is a journey through the labyrinth of relationships after the unthinkable has occurred, a beacon of hope amid the shadows of sorrow.

As a mother, my first instinct was to protect my sons and daughter, to shield him from the crippling pain that consumed us. But grief, I learned, is not a beast to be tamed or hidden away. In the initial weeks and months, it seemed impossible to step back into the world, to face the sympathetic glances and well-meaning words of our friends and social network. Yet, over time, I realized that these connections, once painfully stark reminders of our loss, could be transformed into lifelines of support.

As we journey together through this chapter, my hope is that my experiences and reflections provide you a measure of solace, a beacon to guide your way through the labyrinth. While the path to healing may be arduous and winding, remember, you do not walk it alone.

Communicating with Your Partner

In the tempestuous seas of grief, my family and I found ourselves adrift, unable to chart a course through the swirling storm of our shared sorrow. The ship that was our relationship, once buoyed by love and shared dreams, had been battered by a cruel and unanticipated tempest - the death of our beloved child.

Yet, we found that it wasn't the grief that was drowning us; it was the silence. The tragedy seemed to have muted our ability to communicate, turning us into bystanders of our own suffering. We looked at each other, both desperate to reach out, to find solace, but the words remained trapped behind a wall of pain.

Here are the strategies we adopted in order to rebuild the bridge of communication between us:

• Creating Safe Spaces for Conversation: We began by establishing an environment where it was safe to express our raw emotions, irrespective of how hard they might be to hear or articulate. We designated specific times to share, allowing us to mentally prepare and giving us the security of structure amidst the chaos of our emotions.

• Expressing Grief Individually: Grief is a deeply personal experience, and we each had our unique way of processing it. Recognizing this, we gave each other the space to grieve in our own manner, without imposing our expectations or judgments. This acceptance of our individual grief became a cornerstone of our shared healing process.

• Active Listening: Often, the most powerful healing comes not from words, but from silence. In our conversations, we practiced active listening, focusing on understanding and empathy rather than rushing to offer solutions or advice.

• Using Non-Verbal Communication: When words were too elusive or painful, we turned to non-verbal communication. A gentle touch, a shared tear, a knowing glance - these became our secret language of love and understanding.

• Seeking Professional Help: We realized that our grief was larger than us, and we reached out to a grief counselor. This professional guidance was invaluable in helping us navigate our emotions and communicate more effectively.

• Remembering and Celebrating Our Child: In time, we found comfort in speaking about our child, recounting treasured memories, sharing laughter and tears. These moments, tinged with joy and sorrow, served as a gentle reminder of the love that forever binds us.

The journey of healing is long and winding, and there is no universal roadmap. But communication with your partner can be a powerful compass, guiding you towards shared understanding, empathy, and, eventually, peace. As we opened up to each other, we discovered that our love, resilient and enduring, was our lighthouse amidst the storm.

Supporting Siblings and Family Members

As we wrestled with our own tidal wave of grief, we soon realized that the ripples of our loss had extended far beyond ourselves. My sons and daughter, robbed of their brother, were trapped in their own maelstrom of sorrow, confusion, and fear. Extended family members, grappling with their pain, were unsure of how to support us or address the gaping wound of our loss. Our home was transformed into a sanctuary of silent suffering, each person locked in their solitary battle with grief.

Finding a way to support our surviving child and other family members was a daunting task, a labyrinth within the larger maze of our loss. However, we found that these difficult steps towards support and open communication helped us to not just confront our shared pain, but also to rediscover our shared strength.

• Acknowledging Individual Grief: Just as I was grieving, so too was my younger son, and each of our family members. We learned to respect each person's unique process and timeline, acknowledging their grief without imposing our own expectations on surviving children.

• Promoting Open Communication: We encouraged honest conversation about feelings and fears, reinforcing the fact that it was okay to express these emotions. This included providing a safe space for my sons and daughter to voice their feelings and inviting extended family to share their memories and grief.

• Involving in Memorializing Activities: Together, as a family, we engaged in activities to memorialize our lost child. This included creating a memory box, planting a tree in his honor, and sharing stories about him. This collective activity gave us a shared focus, fostering connection amidst our sorrow.

• Seeking Outside Support: Recognizing that we might not have all the answers or resources to handle this tragic loss, we sought help from grief counselors and support groups. This not only gave us professional guidance but also provided a platform for our surviving children nd other family members to share their feelings with those outside the immediate family circle.

• Maintaining Regular Routines: Amidst the chaos of grief, maintaining regular routines provided a sense of normalcy and security, especially for our younger son. This included school routines, mealtimes, and family activities.

• Celebrating Life: While acknowledging our pain, we also found it important to celebrate life - the life we had lost, the lives we still had, and the love that interconnected us all. This perspective, while difficult to maintain, served as a beacon of hope during our darkest days.

Through these steps, we learned to navigate the rocky terrain of grief together as a family. It was a journey marked by stumbles and setbacks, but also by moments of deep connection and mutual support. While the loss of a child can cast a long shadow over a family, we discovered that within this shadow, we could still find each other - our shared sorrow becoming a bridge, rather than a barrier.

Reconnecting with Friends and Social Networks

The death of a child leaves an indelible mark not only on the immediate family but also on the wider social circle. Friends and acquaintances, once part of our normal routine, may suddenly seem alien, their well-meaning condolences a painful reminder of the depth of our loss. Yet, as we navigated the path of grief, we discovered the importance of reconnecting with these social networks, finding strength and solace in this broader community of support.

The process of reestablishing these connections is not linear, nor is it easy. It is a delicate dance that requires honesty, patience, and sometimes, the courage to set boundaries. Here are the steps we found helpful during this journey:

• Taking the Initiative: When ready, we took the initiative to reach out to our friends. It was hard, but it allowed us to regain some control over our interactions and to set the tone for the conversations.

• Communicating our Needs: Not everyone understands the nature of grief or how to provide support. We found it essential to communicate openly about our feelings, our needs, and what we found comforting or distressing.

• Seeking Out Those Who Listen: We naturally gravitated towards friends who could listen without judgment or unsolicited advice, who could sit with us in our grief rather than trying to 'fix' it.

• Joining Support Groups: Grief support groups, both in-person and online, were invaluable. They provided a safe space to share our experiences, and the community of those who had experienced similar losses was deeply comforting.

• Respecting our Pace: We didn't rush ourselves. Reconnecting with friends and social networks is a gradual process. Some days we felt more sociable; other days, we craved solitude. Both were okay.

• Creating New Rituals: As part of our healing journey, we created new rituals with our friends, such as annual remembrance gatherings, charity events in our child's name, or simply spending time together in nature.

• Learning to Embrace Life Again: It was important for us to learn to enjoy social activities again, without guilt. Laughter and happiness, we realized, were not betrayals of our lost child but a celebration of the love and joy they brought into our lives.

Reconnecting with friends and social networks after the death of a child can feel like trying to fit old pieces into a new puzzle. Yet, it's an important part of the healing process. As we navigated this delicate journey, we found that our relationships, some strained and others strengthened, became a fundamental part of our mosaic of grief and recovery, each piece adding its unique shade to our portrait of healing.

Chapter 4: The Grieving Process for Parents

As we navigate through this journey of healing, it's essential to understand that the grieving process for parents is an intimately personal experience. It's a journey marked by shared sorrow but also individual suffering, shaped by our unique roles, experiences, and responses to the death of a child.

This chapter is dedicated to exploring the diverse facets of parental grief. We'll delve into the specific experiences of mothers, fathers, and single parents, and discuss how these roles and relationships can impact the process of mourning and healing. Though each person's journey is unique, you may find comfort, understanding, and perhaps a sense of solidarity in these shared experiences.

This exploration is not intended to categorize or confine your grief into a specific role. Rather, it's an invitation to better understand the vast landscape of sorrow and healing that stretches before us when we lose a child. By acknowledging these diverse experiences, we can foster a deeper understanding, compassion, and empathy for ourselves and others as we navigate this difficult path.

The Grieving Mother

Losing a child is like having your heart torn out, a wound so deep it feels it will never heal. As a mother, the pain I experienced after the loss of my son was unlike anything I had ever felt before. It was as if a part of my soul had been extinguished, leaving an emptiness that was unbearable.

The relationship between a mother and her child is one of the most intimate bonds in existence. It begins from the moment of conception and continues to grow stronger with each heartbeat, each kick felt in the womb, and every gaze into their eyes. When that bond is severed by death, it feels as though the universe has been ripped apart at the seams.

Emotional Rollercoaster: The grief of a mother is an emotional rollercoaster. One moment I found myself in a state of numbness, a protective shield against the magnitude of my loss. The next, I was consumed by an overwhelming tide of sadness, anger, or guilt. At times, I felt an intense longing to hold my child, to hear his laugh, to comfort him. These emotions would ebb and flow, often without warning, making it difficult to predict or control.

Physical Manifestations: The grief also manifested physically. I experienced fatigue, insomnia, and a loss of appetite. Some days, it felt like an enormous effort just to get out of bed. I learned that it's crucial to listen to your body during these times and give it the care it needs, even when it feels impossible to do so.

Self-Identity: My identity as a mother was also shaken. Mothers are caregivers, nurturers, protectors. So, when a child dies, it challenges that identity. I found myself grappling with questions like, "Am I still a mother? How can I be a mother when my child is not here?"

Nurturing Others: As a mother, I felt an inherent need to nurture and care for others, even in the midst of my grief. I found some solace in taking care of my youngest son, since he was the only one still at home, but it was also tinged with guilt - was I neglecting my lost child's memory by caring for his brother?

Self-Compassion: One of the most important lessons I learned during this time was the importance of self-compassion. As mothers, we often tend to put others' needs before our own. But it's important to remember that your grief matters, your emotions are valid, and it's okay to prioritize your own healing.

Support System: A robust support system can make a significant difference. For me, this was a mix of close family, friends, support groups, and professional counselors. They helped me understand that I was not alone in my grief, provided a safe space to express my feelings, and guided me towards resources and strategies for coping.

My journey as a grieving mother is far from over. It's a path marked with tears and heartache, but also with love, resilience, and moments of grace. It is my hope that in sharing my experience, other mothers facing this unimaginable loss might feel less alone and more understood in their own journeys of grief and healing.

The world doesn't look the same after you've lost a child. Places you frequented with your child can transform from spaces of joy to rooms echoing with the memories of a presence that is no longer there. Even familiar faces can be painful reminders of the loss. Yet, over time, I found that these same spaces could become sanctuaries of solace, where I allowed myself to feel close to my son, remembering the love and joy we shared.

Guilt is another complex emotion that a grieving mother can face. It's not rational, but it's very real. Despite knowing that I could not have foreseen or prevented my son's death, I found myself consumed by "what if" scenarios and guilt for not having been able to protect him. I've come to understand that this guilt is a manifestation of the deep love I hold for my child, the instinctive desire to shield him from harm.

Despite the tremendous pain, there are moments of unexpected grace in this journey. In my case, it's in the way my son's life continues to touch others, in the lessons of love, resilience, and compassion I've learned from this loss, and in the way it's brought me to a deeper understanding of the preciousness of life. These are the moments that provide glimmers of light in the darkness of grief.

The grieving process for a mother can be long and nonlinear, filled with setbacks and small victories. Some days, the fog of grief seems to lift slightly, allowing moments of peace or even joy to sneak in. Other days, it descends back with a crushing weight. It's important to remember that there is no set timetable for grief, and it's okay to have good days and bad days.

It's also important to allow yourself the space to grieve in your own way. Everyone's journey through grief is unique, and what works for one person might not work for another. For me, writing has been a therapeutic outlet, a way to articulate my feelings and memories, and keep my son's spirit alive.

In sharing my journey as a grieving mother, I hope that other mothers walking a similar path might find some comfort. Know that you are not alone, and it's okay to grieve, to hurt, and to heal at your own pace. Your love for your child is eternal, and so is their love for you. Even in the face of such a huge loss, that bond remains unbroken.

The Grieving Father

The grief that fathers endure is a narrative frequently underemphasized within societal discourses of loss. The widely held belief that men, as pillars of strength and resilience, must shoulder everyone's burden during crises is far from reality. Fathers, much like mothers, experience profound sorrow and a deep sense of loss when they lose a child.

It's important to remember that as individuals, these fathers are not merely stoic figures of support; they grapple with the raw, overwhelming emotions that accompany such a tragic event— denial, anger, guilt, and an immense, indescribable sorrow. Even amid their grief, they often strive to portray themselves as the 'strong' ones for their families, even at the cost of their own emotional wellbeing.

This heart-wrenching situation is exacerbated when fathers feel obligated to bear the grief of others while dealing with their own. It can often feel like they are solitary islands in a tumultuous sea, persistently attempting to withstand their own emotional storm while preventing the waves from reaching their loved ones.

Societal norms add further pressure to these grieving fathers, compelling them to return to work and a semblance of 'normalcy' sooner than they are emotionally ready. This can impose a daunting burden, intensifying feelings of loss and disconnection. Fathers are often seen caught in this painful struggle, torn between the pressing need to continue their lives and the profound grief that persists within them.

It's essential to highlight that many families, such as single mothers and their children, rely on these fathers for emotional and practical support. For instance, consider a single mother who, upon losing her eldest child, had to cope not only with her own grief but also support her youngest son, who viewed his deceased elder brother as a father figure. The son, barely fifteen at the time, struggled with his own sorrow while also dealing with the loss of a guiding figure. All this while the mother is still navigating the pain from losing her husband years prior. These multifaceted dynamics underscore the crucial roles fathers play and the unique pressures they face while grieving.

The grieving father's journey is a path through profound pain, societal expectations, personal healing, and the quest for meaning in the aftermath of loss. It's a path that requires immense courage and vulnerability. It's a testament to a father's enduring love for his child.

The grieving process for a father, like a mother, is a nonlinear journey, with its own rhythms and timings. There are moments of healing and moments of deep pain. Understanding and acknowledging this journey is a vital part of healing.

Fathers, your grief is valid, and your loss profound. Your path of grief and healing is unique to you. Know that it's okay to grieve, to reach out, to cry, and to heal. It's okay to lean on others, to share your pain. You don't need to navigate this journey alone. And most importantly, remember that your love for your child and their love for you is an eternal bond that remains unbroken, even by death.

The Grieving Single Parent

Grieving as a single parent is a unique experience marked by layers of complexity. When your child dies, you lose a part of your soul, your heart, and your existence. You lose a part of your identity, your role as a parent to that child. And as a single parent, the loss can feel magnified because of the absence of a co-parent to share in the grief and the memories.

I was a single parent when I lost my son, and I walked alongside friends who had been in this painful place. I have shared their unique struggles, and through them, I know and understand the isolation, overwhelming sorrow, and sheer magnitude of loss that a grieving single parent experience.

A single parent who loses a child we often must grapple with the loneliness and isolation that comes with grief. We must mourn alone, without a partner to hold your hand, to share in your tears, or to simply sit with you in silence. We must bear the pain of loss on our own shoulders, and at the same time, try to comfort and reassure any other children you might have.

The quiet moments at home can be overwhelmingly deafening, each ticking of the clock a stark reminder of the loss you've endured. The duties and responsibilities that we once shared with our child become a painful reminder of their absence. Every corner of your home, every mundane task, holds a memory that tugs at your heart.

Despite experiencing profound pain, myself, I've found a remarkable resilience as a single parent in mourning. I've managed to channel my grief into becoming a stronger version of myself. This journey has taught me that even in the darkest moments, there exist opportunities for growth and healing.

For many grieving single parents, the process of healing is deeply personal and individual. Some find comfort in rituals that honor their child, like visiting their child's favorite places or continuing traditions that were important to their child. Others find solace in support groups, connecting with those who are navigating similar journeys of loss.

Being a grieving single parent is an enduring testament to human strength and the boundless love of a parent. It is a journey marked by profound sadness, but also by moments of reflection, connection, and hope. It's a journey of navigating the world alone while carrying an immense love for a child who will forever be in your heart.

Remember, you don't have to walk this journey alone. Reach out to friends, family, support groups, or grief counselors. Grieve in your own way, in your own time. There's no right or wrong way to grieve, and there's no timetable for grief. And most importantly, remember that you are not alone. There are others who understand your pain, who can offer support, comfort, and understanding. Hold on to the love you have for your child and know that it will be a guiding light through the darkest days of your grief.

Chapter 5: Finding Support in the Midst of Grief

In the darkest hours following my son's passing, the world felt like an unforgiving and desolate place. I found myself yearning for refuge, for an understanding shoulder to lean on, for a hand to guide me through the unbearable pain. This yearning led me to various forms of support - grief counseling, support groups, and the comfort of loved ones. Each played a crucial role in my healing process, providing the strength, resilience, and hope needed to face each day.

Grief Counseling and Therapy

The days after the dreadful news felt like a haze. I moved from moment to moment, a mere ghost navigating through the currents of life. My heart was a gaping wound, the pain so raw, so intense, that it felt unbearable. The silence of my son's room was a deafening reminder of the reality I was trying to escape from. I was lost in a labyrinth of pain and confusion.

That's when I realized I needed help. I couldn't do this alone.

I remember the first time I walked into a grief counselor's office. I was nervous, unsure of what to expect. It felt strange to open up to a stranger about the most devastating experience of my life. But as I began to share, I felt a weight starting to lift off my chest. It was a slow, gradual process, but the sessions with my counselor proved to be an anchor in the turbulent sea of my grief.

Grief counseling offered a safe and non-judgmental space where I could express my deepest fears, my guilt, my anger, and the myriad of other emotions that came with the loss. The counselor was not just a passive listener. She helped me understand my feelings better, navigate the complex stages of grief, and develop coping mechanisms. She reassured me that what I was going through was normal, that it was okay to feel what I was feeling.

Therapy sessions also equipped me with tools to deal with the physical aspects of grief. We often overlook the fact that grief is not just an emotional journey; it takes a toll on our bodies too. Sleeplessness, loss of appetite, fatigue – these were all part of my experience. My counselor helped me address these issues, emphasizing the importance of self-care during this challenging time.

One significant aspect of grief therapy was the exploration of my relationship with my lost child. We spoke about him – his life, his dreams, our shared moments. Far from making me sadder, these conversations brought me closer to acceptance. I realized that while death had taken my son away from the physical world, he lived on in my memories and heart.

While grief counseling and therapy may not be a magic bullet for the pain, it can be an invaluable resource in the healing journey. It's a personal decision, and what works for one might not work for the other. But for me, it was a lighthouse guiding me through the storm, a sanctuary where I learned to understand my pain, to cope, to survive, and ultimately, to heal.

There were days, however, when I felt that the progress I was making in therapy was too slow or non-existent. Moments of darkness would wash over me, and I would question if I was making any headway at all. My counselor patiently reiterated that grief doesn't follow a linear path. There would be times of regression, of feeling stuck, but it did not mean that I was not moving forward. It was simply the nature of grief.

Grief counseling often incorporated various therapeutic techniques tailored to my individual needs and preferences. Cognitive-behavioral therapy, for instance, helped me recognize negative thought patterns and replace them with healthier ones. Techniques from mindfulness therapy taught me to live in the present, to focus on the here and now rather than becoming engulfed in the past or anxious about the future.

One unexpected but crucial outcome of therapy was the realization of how my loss had affected the people around me. I discovered that my grief, in its overwhelming intensity, had made me somewhat blind to the suffering of others. This proved to be beneficial not just for me but for my whole family. It allowed us to communicate our feelings openly, understand each other's grief, and offer support. It helped us to grieve together, to heal together.

Another vital aspect of therapy was the discussion of grief triggers - situations, dates, or objects that could trigger intense grief reactions. Identifying these triggers and learning to manage the emotions they evoked was a crucial step in my healing journey.

Grief counseling doesn't promise to take away the pain or bring back what we have lost. It does, however, provide a roadmap, a guide to walk through the valley of grief with resilience and hope. It helps us embrace our new normal, equips us to deal with the aftermath of loss, and encourages us to find meaning and purpose again.

In my journey of healing, I found grief counseling to be a beacon. It was an investment in my wellbeing, an essential step towards finding my footing in a world that had been irrevocably altered. It didn't make the journey easy, but it made it bearable. It was there in the bleakness, a constant companion, gently nudging me towards a path of healing and acceptance.

Support Groups and Communities

In the aftermath of my son's passing, the loneliness was as profound as the grief. While I had the love and support of my family and friends, I often felt isolated in my suffering. My world had been shattered, yet life around me continued unabated, a constant reminder of the normalcy I had lost. It was during this time of desolation that I found another lifeline: Support groups and grief communities.

While individual therapy was pivotal in my healing journey, joining a support group introduced me to a different facet of the healing process. A support group is essentially a group of individuals who have experienced a similar loss. Coming together in a safe space, they share their experiences, feelings, struggles, and insights, providing mutual support and understanding.

The first support group meeting I attended was overwhelming. The room was filled with parents like me, each carrying the weight of their child's loss. There was a palpable sense of sorrow, but also a sense of solidarity. Here, I was not alone. Here, everyone understood the depth of my pain without me having to explain it. And here, everyone was journeying through the same tumultuous sea of grief, just like me.

In the shared narratives of grief and loss, I found solace and understanding. Every story was unique, yet every story echoed similar sentiments - the shock, the disbelief, the pain, the longing. We shared our experiences, the moments of utter despair, the little victories, the steps backward, the progress forward.

As weeks turned into months, these meetings became a constant in my life. We cried together, remembered our children together, and on good days, even managed to laugh together. We celebrated the lives of our children, shared their stories, and kept their memories alive.

The support group also served as a platform for collective learning. We learned from each other's experiences, sharing strategies to cope, ways to honour our children, and how to navigate sensitive situations like birthdays or anniversaries. Professionals were often invited to these meetings to provide information and insights on various aspects of grief, healing, and mental health.

In this collective grieving, I found a profound sense of healing. It was comforting to know that I was not alone, that my feelings were valid, and that healing, while difficult, was possible. The shared experiences made me feel seen, understood, and acknowledged. It fostered a sense of connection, a connection borne out of shared pain but one that proved to be incredibly comforting and healing.

Online grief communities also became a significant part of my support system. On days when the weight of my loss made leaving the house impossible, I found comfort in online forums, blogs, and social media groups. These virtual platforms offered a space to share and connect with others, irrespective of the time or day.

Grief, as I learned, does not follow a timetable. There were nights when sleep seemed impossible, when the loss felt as fresh as it was on day one. During such times, these online spaces provided immediate solace. I could share my feelings, read about others who were going through the same, or just scroll through the messages and posts, drawing comfort from the fact that others understood my pain.

Support groups and communities, both offline and online, played an integral role in my healing journey. They gave me a sense of belonging, a sense of being understood, and a sense of hope. They reminded me that while the journey of grief was undoubtedly a lonely one, I didn't have to walk it alone. There were others on the same path, each navigating their own course, but together, we could support and uplift each other. In their companionship, I found strength, resilience, and the courage to keep going.

While every individual's journey of grief is unique, and different forms of support work for different people, I found solace in these groups. I found a community. I found understanding. And in many ways, I found a way to channel my grief into something that made me feel a little less alone, a little more understood, and a little closer to healing. It was not a substitute for my loss, but it was a balm for my grieving heart. For those navigating the turbulent waters of child loss, such support groups and communities can indeed be a beacon of hope in the dark journey of grief.

Art and Creative Expression in Healing

When words fell short, and the agony of grief felt too overwhelming to articulate, I discovered a new avenue of expressing my pain: art. Creative expression became an integral part of my healing journey, a refuge where I could bare my soul and manifest my grief in a tangible form.

Art, in its many forms, provided a canvas where the colors of my emotions could dance freely. It was not about creating masterpieces, but about the process itself, the act of pouring out the chaos within me and giving it form. Here are some forms of art and creative expression that can be employed in the healing journey:

Painting and Drawing: Picking up a paintbrush or a pencil allowed me to express my feelings visually. The blank canvas was a silent, non-judgmental companion that bore witness to the spectrum of my emotions – the blues of my sorrow, the reds of my anger, the grays of my despair. Each stroke was a word unsaid, a tear unshed, a sigh unheaved.

Sculpture or Pottery: Working with clay or other materials to create sculptures can be a therapeutic way to channel grief. The tactile nature of these art forms can be grounding and the act of creating something can give a sense of accomplishment and control, which can be helpful when navigating the chaotic emotions of grief.

Writing and Poetry: Pouring my thoughts onto paper became a powerful tool in my journey. Writing letters to my lost son, penning down my feelings in a grief journal, composing poetry – these were cathartic experiences. It was a safe space where my deepest fears, regrets, and longings could coexist with my memories, gratitude, and love.

Music: Whether it was playing an instrument, singing, or just listening to songs that resonated with my feelings, music proved to be a great source of comfort. It had the power to reflect and validate my emotions, and at times, provide a release for them.

Photography: Capturing moments, sights, or objects that resonated with my feelings was another form of creative expression. It was not about the aesthetics but the emotions that the images encapsulated.

Dance or Movement Therapy: Expressing emotions through body movement can be incredibly freeing. Dancing, even in solitude, allowed me to physically express and release the tension, sorrow, and other emotions that often felt trapped in my body.

Crafts: Simple activities like making a scrapbook of memories, crafting a piece of jewelry, knitting, or building a small memorial can also serve as outlets for grief.

Each form of creative expression served as a language when words felt inadequate. There was no judgement, no rules, no right or wrong. It was just me, my grief, and a medium to channel it. The rawness of my pain was given a form – visible, tangible, real.

Engaging in art allowed me to witness my grief outside of myself, to view it from a different perspective. It also helped me communicate my grief to others when words felt insufficient. Sharing my creations gave others a glimpse into my journey, building understanding and empathy.

The most beautiful aspect of using art in my healing journey was that it kept my son's memory alive. I could paint our shared moments, write about our conversations, create a melody inspired by his laughter. Through art, I was not just expressing my grief, but also celebrating my son's life, our bond, and the love that remained.

In essence, the therapeutic nature of art and creative expression can play a vital role in the journey of grief and healing. It doesn't require professional skills or talent - just an open heart willing to express its vulnerability. It's about finding a form of expression that resonates with you, giving voice to your pain, and in the process, fostering understanding, empathy, and healing. It's about transforming your grief into a testament of your love, your loss, and your resilience.

Art also provided an outlet for the accumulation of unexpressed emotions, those feelings that were too complex or overwhelming to articulate. I was able to visualize my sorrow, my longing, my love, my memories - they all found a place on my canvas, in my poetry, or within the notes of my music. It was as if the creative process helped decompress my heavy heart, giving each emotion its rightful place and recognition.

Moreover, art opened up a dialogue with myself. It compelled me to confront my feelings, to delve into the depths of my pain, and to understand its layers. I was no longer running from my emotions or suppressing them; I was acknowledging and accepting them through my art.

One surprising outcome of this artistic journey was the discovery of a community. By sharing my art, I connected with others who were walking the same path of loss and grief. We found solace in each other's expressions, comfort in our shared understanding, and strength in our collective resilience. This sense of community was healing in itself.

Importantly, the process of creating art in grief is a highly personal and individual experience. The choice of medium, the pace, the style - everything depends on one's comfort and emotional state. There is no predetermined path or 'right' way to do it. The focus is not on the result but the process - the act of creation itself. It is about expressing what feels unexpressable, making sense of the senseless, and navigating through the overwhelming storm of grief.

Furthermore, there is no time limit to this process. Grief is not a linear journey with a defined endpoint. It is a long winding road with its ups and downs, its calm days, and its stormy nights. Similarly, the use of art as a tool in the healing process is not confined to a specific time frame. It can be a companion in the early days of raw grief, a solace in the later stages when the world moves on, and a comfort even years down the line when the loss has been woven into the fabric of one's existence.

Creativity in the face of grief may seem like a paradox, but it is a testament to the human spirit's resilience. It represents the potential for beauty to emerge from our deepest sorrows, and for healing to occur in the most unexpected of places. It is a powerful reminder that even in our darkest hours, we have within us the ability to express, connect, and ultimately, heal. It may not ease the pain instantly, nor will it fill the void left by loss, but it can provide a lifeline, a medium to understand, cope, and navigate the turbulent seas of grief.

In the end, art, in whatever form it may take, becomes more than just an activity; it becomes a sanctuary, a testament of one's journey through grief. It stands as a monument to the love that endures, the memories that persist, and the healing that is possible, even in the face of loss.

Chapter 6: Coping with Your New Future

It's been said that when a child dies, a part of the parent dies too. This raw, unfathomable reality of life after the loss of a child can leave us in a world that feels alien, irreconcilable with the life we knew before. This chapter explores the challenging but crucial journey of coping with this new future, as we seek to reconcile our immense grief with the relentless passage of time. We delve into the emotional landscape of reimagining our life after such a loss, finding ways to redirect the pain into purpose, and slowly allowing ourselves to hope and heal.

As we peel back the layers of grief, we encounter fresh aspects of our altered reality. From redefining our identity outside of the parenthood that was so brutally taken from us, to rediscovering purpose and meaning in a world that has shifted on its axis, the journey is anything but linear. Yet, amidst the chaos, we also catch glimpses of resilience, a testament to the enduring spirit of parenthood, even after death.

It is in these moments of reflection, acceptance, and growth that we start to embrace the possibilities of hope and healing. Our child's absence etches a permanent mark on our soul, but it's through this profound sorrow that we learn to navigate our new existence. This chapter sheds light on this transformative journey, offering a beacon of support and understanding for those walking this heartrending path.

Reimagining Your Life After Loss

There's a certain pattern to life that we all follow, almost unconsciously, like a generation of monarch butterflies traveling thousands of miles, instinctively knowing the path. But when a child's life is abruptly taken away, it feels as if we are forced off that path into an uncharted wilderness, abandoned and disoriented. The generation you were a part of - parenthood - feels like it has become insufficient, incomplete. And yet, the world keeps moving forward, oblivious to your pain, leaving you stranded in the stark reality of your child's absence. Here lies the crux of our journey in this section: to learn how to navigate this wilderness, to reimagine our life in the wake of this loss.

Admittedly, reimagining your life after losing a child is not an overnight task. It is a slow, deliberate process of acceptance and transformation. It's about acknowledging the void and then, gradually filling it with new experiences, while keeping the memories of your child alive. It's about learning to draw strength from your pain, allowing it to reshape you, and finally letting it guide you towards a life that you can still find meaningful.

The concept of 'moving on to the next generation' can be daunting. After all, how does one even begin to imagine a future without their child in it? It's a difficult question and yet, it's one we must face. This does not mean forgetting or replacing. Instead, it's about finding ways to carry your child's memory forward, integrating their legacy into your life and the lives of those around you. This can take various forms. Some people may choose to honor their child's memory by contributing to causes their child cared about, others might find solace in creating art, writing, or music inspired by their child.

This shift does not negate the reality of your loss, nor does it undermine the love you hold for your child. On the contrary, it serves as a testament to that love, a way to allow their spirit to continue to be a part of your life, while simultaneously granting you the space to heal and find joy again.

Remember, there is no prescribed path or timeline for this process. Every journey is unique, every parent will find their own way. In this wilderness, we learn to navigate by intuition and need, making our own trail. As we inch forward, slowly but resolutely, we begin to reimagine a life where grief and joy can coexist. This is not about leaving behind, but about carrying forward, about learning to live again while honoring our child's life and legacy. It's a testament to our resilience, a love letter to our lost child, and a brave step towards our new future.

The transformation after the loss of a child does not happen in isolation. It is a journey shared with those around you who also loved your child, and who carry their own grief. You find yourself not only grappling with your personal sorrow but also bearing witness to the grief of siblings, grandparents, friends, and even your community. This shared pain, while profoundly hard, can also be a source of mutual understanding and support.

Shared grief, however, does not mean identical grief. Every person's relationship with your child was unique, and so too will be their grieving process. A brother might act out in anger, a sister that may go wild or spiral into a depression, a grandparent might retreat into silence, a friend might seem to move on more quickly than you expected. These differences can be challenging to navigate, but they also offer opportunities for deep empathy and connection.

One of the key things to remember is that communication becomes crucial during this time. Expressing your feelings and listening to others express theirs can bring comfort and connection. It allows you to understand and respect each other's unique experiences of grief and offers a shared language for this new reality.

As you move forward, you may find that some relationships change, and new ones may form. People who were once on the periphery of your life might step forward in unexpected ways, while others may pull away, unable to deal with the enormity of the loss. This reshuffling of relationships can be disconcerting, but it can also lead to deep and meaningful connections built on shared grief and mutual support.

Throughout this process, self-care is crucial. This is not a selfish act, but rather, a necessary part of your healing journey. Giving yourself permission to rest, to seek comfort, and to express your feelings, without judgment, can help you navigate this difficult time. You might find solace in nature, in quiet moments of reflection, or in the company of a trusted friend or family member. What matters is that you allow yourself the space and time to heal in your own way, at your own pace.

Finally, as you navigate this terrain of shared grief and evolving relationships, you may find that your role within your family and community shifts. You might become a source of strength for others, a conduit for expressing and understanding grief, and a keeper of your child's memory. This shift can be profound, but it can also bring a sense of purpose and continuity, as you carry your child's legacy forward into the future. You may find, in time, that you have not only reimagined your life but also transformed it, carving out a place of honor for your child within the tapestry of your new existence.

Rediscovering Purpose and Meaning

Moving through the loss of a child, one may feel as though life's purpose and meaning have been extinguished. The world, once vibrant and full of possibility, can seem utterly void and meaningless, making every task feel like an insurmountable mountain. This is normal, a part of the grieving process, but it's crucial to remember that this darkness is not your destination. The journey of grief, though fraught with pain, is also a pathway to rediscovery.

Reframing your reality takes time, patience, and kindness towards oneself. It's like slowly emerging from a dense fog, where shapes and colors start to regain their form, albeit differently than before. It is about reorienting yourself in a world irrevocably changed, where your sense of self and purpose have to be renegotiated.

• Connect with your inner strength: One of the ways you can start rediscovering purpose is by connecting with the resilient part of yourself that has carried you this far. Recognize your strength, resilience, and capacity for love. It is there, even if it feels buried deep beneath your sorrow.

• Seek solace in rituals: Establishing small, personal rituals can be very therapeutic. They can serve as a touchstone of comfort and a way to honor your child's memory. A ritual could be as simple as lighting a candle, visiting a cherished location, or playing their favorite song. These actions can provide a sense of continuity and connection, even amid profound loss.

• Embrace your passions: Embracing your passions and interests can be a powerful tool for rediscovery. Whether it's painting, gardening, running, or any other activity that you love, giving yourself permission to engage with these activities can bring a sense of joy and purpose back into your life.

• Seek support: Grief can often feel isolating, but you don't have to journey through it alone. Reach out to supportive friends, family members, or seek professional help. Speaking about your experiences and feelings can provide much-needed perspective and validation.

Rediscovering purpose and meaning is not about forgetting or moving past the loss. It's about learning to carry the weight of that loss while also making space for growth, joy, and continued life. It's about weaving the memory of your child into your life's tapestry, honoring their presence in your new normal.

It's a process, a journey, not a destination, and it unfolds in its own time, at its own pace. Remember, it's okay to stumble, it's okay to fall. What matters is that you keep going, keep growing, keep living. Your life, even in its most painful moments, holds infinite value and potential for joy.

Embracing Hope and Healing

Now we arrive at a crucial juncture in your journey — embracing hope and healing. To some, the very idea might seem like a far-off dream, even an impossibility. How can one possibly harbor hope after such a profound loss? How does one heal when the wound feels like an abyss? This section isn't about providing an instant remedy or promising a pain-free future; instead, it aims to illuminate the path towards a future where grief and joy, sorrow and hope, can coexist.

Every dawn, as the sun breaks over the horizon, it brings with it the promise of a new day. This is hope. It's not about forgetting the night or dismissing the darkness; it's about acknowledging the light that follows. Embracing hope after the death of a child isn't about negating your pain or replacing your loss; it's about recognizing that alongside your grief, life can still contain moments of beauty, joy, and love.

The transition towards hope and healing can begin with tiny, tentative steps. You might start by merely allowing yourself to imagine a future where you can breathe a little easier, laugh a little louder, live a little fuller. Then, gradually, you work towards this future, one day at a time.

Healing, like grief, is not linear. There will be setbacks and difficult days. Healing doesn't mean the pain completely vanishes, but rather it changes in its intensity and frequency over time. It means that over time, the good days start outnumbering the bad ones.

• Allow yourself to hope: Allow yourself to imagine a future where your heart isn't as heavy, where joy doesn't feel like a betrayal. It doesn't mean you love or miss your child any less; it simply means you're allowing life to continue alongside your loss.

• Practice self-care: Prioritize your physical and emotional well-being. Exercise, proper nutrition, sufficient sleep, meditation, and relaxation techniques can significantly influence your mental and emotional health.

• Seek therapy and support groups: Professional help and support from those who've experienced similar losses can be immensely beneficial. Sharing your journey, hearing others' stories, and realizing you're not alone can aid healing.

• Celebrate the life lived: Honor your child's life and the love you shared by continuing to celebrate their memory. This can take numerous forms and will be unique to each person. By keeping their memory alive, you're inviting healing into your life.

• Take your time: Everyone's timeline for healing is different. Do not rush yourself or let others rush you. Healing cannot be hurried.

Embracing hope and healing is about giving yourself permission to live a life that still holds potential for happiness, even after such a profound loss. It's about accepting that your hearth will always carry this sorrow, it also has the capacity to hold joy, love, and hope in the same sacred space. Do not give up, your child would not want that for you; do not let the numbness from grief control your future. Remember your child is who you must go on and live a life they would be proud of.

Chapter 7: Honoring Your Child's Memory

The sun had set, but the darkness could not shroud the light that was my son's spirit. His death had torn a gaping wound in my heart, a wound I was still learning to navigate. Yet, amidst the storm of sorrow, a new chapter was dawning on my path of healing - a chapter dedicated to honoring the radiant legacy my child left behind. This was the spark that inspired me to keep going, to wake up each day and choose to remember him not just in death, but in the vibrant life he led.

This chapter explores the sacred journey of honoring your child's memory. It's a labyrinth of emotions, a bittersweet mix of mourning and celebration. Here, we delve into the creation of memorials and tributes, crafting tangible tokens of love that keep the connection to your child vibrant and present. We will navigate through rituals and traditions, those intimate threads woven through our everyday lives that help us remember, cherish, and celebrate our child's essence.

Lastly, we'll discuss ways to keep your child's legacy alive, a beacon that continues to illuminate our path even when they are physically absent. This chapter is an invitation to seek solace in remembering, a tender reminder that love transcends the physical realm and our connections to our children can continue to evolve, even after their departure.

Creating a Memorial or Tribute

As we step into the territory of memory, the generation of the past may sometimes feel insufficient to hold the entirety of our child's life, their dreams, their laughter, and the singular way they touched our world. The spaces they once filled with their energy may echo with their absence, making us feel as though we are standing on the edge of a precipice, staring into a void that was once their vibrant existence. In such moments, we may find it healing to create something tangible, a tribute or memorial that can serve as a bridge across this void, connecting us to the beautiful legacy they left behind.

Creating a memorial or tribute doesn't need to be grandiose or elaborate; it simply needs to reflect the essence of your child and the unique bond you shared. This could take the form of a physical shrine in a quiet corner of your home, adorned with their pictures, favorite belongings, or little mementos that echo with their personality. A favorite toy, a piece of jewelry they cherished, or even a drawing they once made could serve as a tribute to their spirit.

On the other hand, you might find solace in creating a tribute that can be shared with others. This could be a digital memorial, a website or a social media page dedicated to their memory, filled with photos, anecdotes, and expressions of love from family, friends, and all those whose lives they touched. The choice of medium is personal, what matters is that it resonates with your way of remembering and celebrating your child.

Alternatively, a tribute could also take the form of an event or activity. Organizing a charity event, a scholarship in their name, or a local community project that aligns with their passions or interests are wonderful ways to honor your child's memory. These tributes not only preserve their legacy but also allow their spirit to continue making a positive impact on the world.

Creating a memorial or tribute can be a profoundly therapeutic process. As we gather fragments of our child's life, weaving them into a tapestry of remembrance, we also learn to navigate the currents of our grief. This journey may evoke a river of tears, but it may also kindle a warm, inner smile as we remember the joy, the love, and the light our children brought into our lives. As we venture into this process, we are not just constructing a tribute to them; we are also building a bridge between generations - a bridge of love, of memory, and of the enduring spirit of our beloved child.

As we continue to navigate through the labyrinth of emotions that constitute this journey, it's important to remember that it's okay to seek help and collaborate with others. Engaging family members or friends who also cherished your child can be a deeply moving and healing experience. They can contribute their unique memories, moments, and insights, enriching the narrative and breadth of the tribute. Through these shared efforts, you can collectively breathe life into your child's legacy, highlighting the multifaceted impact they had on the people around them.

There's a kind of magic in this communal remembering, a comforting reminder that your child was deeply loved, and their life had significance that reached beyond the confines of the family. Creating a shared space for people to express their grief and love can become a cathartic process, a salve to the communal wound left by your child's absence.

Furthermore, you might find healing in creating something with your own hands - a craft project, a piece of art, or even a scrapbook filled with mementos. These personal, tangible expressions of love and remembrance are more than just objects; they are vessels that carry your emotions, your connection, your love for your child. They serve as a beacon of their presence, an embodiment of their spirit.

Consider also, the possibility of an evolving tribute. You could plant a tree in your child's honor, a living testament to their memory. Each year as it grows, it stands as a symbol of their enduring presence in your life, the roots delving deeper into the soil just as your child's influence continues to permeate your being. The blossoms and leaves might serve as a reminder of the cyclical nature of life and the beauty that persists even amid pain.

The process of creating a memorial or tribute is deeply personal and unique to each individual. There is no single correct way to go about it. Listen to your heart. Honor your own pace. Some days might be harder than others, and that's okay. The goal isn't to create a perfect tribute, but to craft a space that feels safe and comforting, a space where you can feel close to your child. In this process, you're not just commemorating your child's existence; you're also nurturing your own healing, moving from one generation of grief to the next, slowly but surely finding your way through the sorrow.

Rituals and Traditions

Just as we began to craft our tribute, there was a dawning realization that the process of healing was not limited to tangible objects or grand gestures. As I moved further along my journey of grief, I discovered a new layer of connection, found in the smallest of moments and most ordinary of days. The ritual of making his favorite pancakes on a Sunday morning, or quietly celebrating his love for space exploration during the annual Perseid meteor shower. These rituals and traditions, whether new or old, became sacred touchstones, grounding me amidst the whirlwind of my loss.

In the beginning, the rituals might seem daunting, reminders of a life that was but is no more. We might fear that by indulging in them, we'd be reopening old wounds. However, with time and patience, these very rituals can transform into gentle bridges, leading us back to the connection we had with our child, enabling us to hold their memory close.

Here are some ways you could incorporate rituals and traditions into your journey:

Shared meals: Prepare your child's favorite meal on significant days or whenever you miss them. The act of cooking, of filling your kitchen with the aromas they loved can feel like an intimate act of remembrance, a moment of sharing that transcends the physical plane.

Personal artifacts: Wear a piece of jewelry or clothing that belonged to them. It could serve as a comforting reminder of their presence, a tangible connection that you can carry with you.

Celebrate their passions: Engage in activities or hobbies they loved. Whether it was painting, hiking, or watching old movies, immersing yourself in their passions can feel like a shared experience, a window into their world.

Anniversary traditions: Mark the anniversary of their passing in a way that feels meaningful to you. This could be as simple as lighting a candle, visiting their resting place, or spending the day in a place they loved.

Symbolic gestures: Find a symbolic gesture that resonates with you. It could be releasing balloons on their birthday, planting flowers in their honor, or even just looking up at their favorite constellation in the night sky.

Each of these rituals carries its own rhythm, its own silent melody that whispers of love, connection, and remembrance. They need not be grand or elaborate; instead, they should be authentic reflections of your relationship with your child. They might bring tears to your eyes, but they may also bring a soft smile to your lips as you remember the love, the joy, and the shared moments that tie you to your child.

As we journey deeper into the heart of our rituals and traditions, we may find an unexpected ally in the changing seasons. Every autumn leaf might remind us of our child's love for October's riot of colors. The first snowfall could echo with their laughter, a sound we thought was lost in the depths of our memory. Even the dawn of spring, with its renewal of life, might speak to us of our child's unquenchable spirit, their irrepressible zest for life.

These small acts, carried out in the rhythm of the changing seasons, can become our personal traditions. They are a testament to the enduring love we hold for our child. As we watch the leaves fall, we can whisper their name into the wind. As the first snowflakes descend, we can share in their joy, and come spring, we can celebrate their life amidst the bloom of flowers. These traditions tether us to the cyclical nature of life and death, a reminder that love, like the seasons, persists despite the changes. In crafting these rituals, we might find comfort in solitude, or we might invite others who loved our child to join us.

Sharing these traditions with siblings, family members, or close friends can create a communal space for grief and remembrance. For instance, gathering on your child's birthday to share memories, stories, or just sit in silence can become a cherished tradition. Through these shared moments, our child's life continues to touch others, weaving an enduring tapestry of love and connection.

Let's also remember that our child's belongings can become integral parts of these rituals. Their favorite book, a treasured baseball cap, or even their beloved playlist can be woven into our daily routine. By incorporating these elements, we not only honor our child's memory, but we also keep a piece of them alive in our everyday life.

Above all, these rituals and traditions are your safe haven, a place where you can freely express your love, your grief, and everything in between. They are the lighthouses in the stormy sea of loss, guiding us towards healing. These rituals remind us that our love for our child is not bound by their physical presence. It is an enduring bond, one that continues to thrive and evolve, even as we navigate the waters of loss. They help us understand that while we may have lost our child in one generation, their memory persists, lovingly preserved in the rituals and traditions that celebrate their life.

Keeping Your Child's Legacy Alive

The quest to preserve my child's legacy wasn't solely an endeavor of mourning, but also a labor of love, a testament to their irreplaceable place in our lives. In the quiet moments of solitude, in the heartrending instances of longing, I sought to keep his spirit alive, not just as a memory of the past, but as an integral part of my present, and an inspiration for the future.

Creating a legacy, much like creating a tribute or crafting rituals, is an intimately personal journey. It's not about grandiose gestures or public recognition, but about honoring your child's individuality, their passions, and the footprints they left in the hearts of those who knew them.

Here are some ways to keep your child's legacy alive:

Share Their Stories: Start by sharing their stories, their dreams, their quirks, and their kindness. Each tale is a brushstroke in the painting of their life, a testament to their unique spirit. Write these stories down in a journal, share them with family and friends, or even create a blog or social media page dedicated to their memory.

Continue Their Work: If they had a passion project or a cause they were devoted to, consider carrying on their work. It could be as simple as maintaining a garden they loved or as impactful as continuing their volunteer work or advocacy.

Create a Scholarship: If you have the means, establishing a scholarship in their name at their school or college is a meaningful way to honor their passion for learning and help other students.

Donate or Volunteer: Consider donating to a charity they believed in or volunteering at an organization they loved. Not only will you be helping others, but you'll also be honoring your child's values.

Live Their Values: Above all, strive to live the values that your child embodied. If they were compassionate, make an effort to be kinder. If they were curious, explore the world with wide-eyed wonder. Let their life continue to inspire and guide you.

Remember, there is no set path or timeframe for creating a legacy. It might take weeks, months, or even years before you feel ready, and that's perfectly fine. Your child's legacy isn't defined by the speed at which it's established, but by the love and honor that permeates every effort.

As I embarked on this journey to keep my child's legacy alive, I realized that it was more than a symbolic act; it was a transformative process. It helped me view my child's life not just through the lens of loss, but as a lasting source of inspiration, love, and connection. Keeping his legacy alive meant that his spirit continued to thrive, bringing a sense of purpose, healing, and even joy amidst the sorrow.

In the process of honoring my child's legacy, I discovered that the flame of his life continued to burn brightly, illuminating my path as I journeyed through the wilderness of grief. In his memory, I found strength, resilience, and a profound sense of love that defied the boundaries of life and death. His legacy became a beacon, guiding me through the darkness, and reminding me that even in loss, his life continued to unfold, touching hearts, inspiring change, and forever shaping the world in ways both seen and unseen.

In the tapestry of our everyday life, the thread of our child's legacy can be beautifully woven. As I went about my daily routines, I found that each act, each decision could be a tribute to my son, keeping his essence alive in the most ordinary moments. Each time I chose to be patient, each time I opted for kindness, each time I embraced his love for the environment by nurturing my garden, I could feel his legacy being etched deeper into the fabric of my life.

Often, it's in these simple acts of living that we can celebrate our child in the most authentic way. Perhaps it's by cooking their favorite meal, using less plastic in honor of their love for the environment, or even adopting their habit of reading before bedtime. As we integrate these fragments of their life into ours, we not only honor their legacy but also allow it to evolve and grow with us.

If your child was artistic, maybe you could express their legacy through art. Create paintings, write poems, or compose music that reflects their spirit. If they loved nature, plant a tree in their memory or adopt a park. Such acts not only keep our child's memory alive but also contribute positively to our communities, extending their impact beyond the immediate sphere of family and friends.

You might also consider creating a digital memorial for your child. This can be a dedicated website or a social media page where people can share memories, photos, and stories. It can serve as a communal space for collective mourning and remembrance, a testament to the lives they touched.

Yet, the most profound way to honor your child's legacy is to allow yourself to heal, to live, and to find joy again. Your happiness does not diminish the depth of your loss or the love you hold for your child. Instead, it is a tribute to them, a testament to the strength of the human spirit that they were a part of. Remember, your child's legacy is intricately tied to you, and as you heal, you allow their legacy to shine brighter.

Keeping your child's legacy alive is not a task to be completed but a journey to be embraced. It's about keeping their spirit close, allowing it to inspire and guide us as we navigate our life. As I found, the journey might be painful at times, filled with longing and tears, but it's also imbued with love, resilience, and a deep sense of connection that transcends the physical realm. In honoring their legacy, we keep a part of our child alive within us, a spark that continues to illuminate our path, making our journey through grief a little less lonely, a little more bearable.

Chapter 8: Navigating Special Dates and Anniversaries

Grief is an unwelcome guest that never truly leaves, but there are times when its presence feels more pronounced, heavier. Special dates and anniversaries punctuate the calendar like stars in the night sky - their twinkle is a mix of sweet memories and poignant longing. Birthdays, holidays, the anniversary of the day they left us; these are moments that once brought joy but now hold a mirror to the enormity of our loss. They can reignite grief in a painful, often overwhelming way, making the wound feel as fresh as the day it was inflicted.

But as we navigate this new reality, we must also learn how to traverse these specially marked dates on our calendar. They are part of the healing journey, a testament to the enduring bond of love that death cannot erase. It is in these moments that we remember not only the depth of our loss but the height of our love. How we manage these days can shape our healing journey, providing opportunities for remembrance, release, and resilience.

Birthdays and Anniversaries

Every date on the calendar that holds a connection to our child can feel like a landmine, waiting to detonate our fragile peace. Among the most challenging of these are birthdays and anniversaries - days that have etched themselves into our hearts with the sharp pen of love and loss

For me, it was my son's 21st birthday, a date I had often imagined filled with celebration, laughter, and pride. Instead, I found myself standing in front of his urn, clutching my favorite photograph in Las Vegas with his brother and sister because that is where he was hoping to spend it, the bitter wind howling around me as if reflecting my inner turmoil. The joy of this day had become a somber event, a stark reminder of the cruel twist of fate that took my child away. But in that moment, I also remembered his smile, his laughter, and how much he loved being surprised with a homemade birthday cake.

Moving through these dates can feel like walking through a minefield, but it's important to remember that every step we take is a part of the journey towards healing. This journey, however, is not about forgetting our loved ones or the pain. It's about learning to carry both the love and the loss with grace, acknowledging the sadness while still remembering to celebrate their life.

On these significant days, create a space for your grief and your love. It's okay to shed tears for the birthdays they will never have and the milestones they will never reach. Your sorrow is a testament to your love. But also remember to honor their memory by recalling the joy they brought into your life. You could write them a letter, release a balloon with a message, make their favorite meal, or simply share stories about them with friends and family.

Through these actions, our loved ones continue to be a part of our lives. We carry them in our hearts, in our stories, and in our continued love for them. Remember, there's no right or wrong way to navigate these dates. You must do what feels most comforting to you. These days will always be hard, but with time, they will also become a testament to your resilience, to your capacity to hold both grief and love in your heart, and your ability to forge a path forward, carrying the memory of your child with you always.

Holidays and Family Gatherings

Holidays and family gatherings are often associated with joy, togetherness, and celebration. But after the loss of a child, these occasions can morph into a stark reminder of their absence, casting a long shadow over what used to be a time of joy.

The first Christmas arrived just 18 days after my son passed. However, the usual joy and festivities were absent that year. The ornaments and lights stayed in their boxes, each one carrying a poignant memory of him that we weren't yet ready to confront. It was his star that always crowned the tree, the little angel ornament crafted by his second-grade hands, the tinsel he would drape around himself, pretending to be the real Christmas gift... Each element was an echo of his laughter, his joy, and a stark reminder of his absence. It took a few years before we could even begin to consider celebrating Christmas again, and that was okay. Each one of us was on our own unique journey of grieving and healing.

It is normal to dread these days, to wish that we could skip them or wake up when they are over. But much like birthdays and anniversaries, these challenging days are also a part of our journey through grief and healing. Here are a few thoughts on how to navigate these emotionally charged times:

Prepare in Advance: Anticipating the difficulty of these occasions can help you in managing your emotions. Think about what traditions you might want to keep, change, or let go. You might also want to communicate your feelings and needs with your family and friends to prepare them and request their support.

It's OK to Say No: You don't have to attend every gathering or event. Give yourself permission to say no to invitations if you feel that it would be too hard for you.

Create a New Tradition: This can be a way to remember and honor your child. It could be something as simple as lighting a candle, sharing favorite stories, or even cooking their favorite dish.

Seek Support: Surround yourself with people who understand and respect your grief. You might also find comfort in connecting with others who have experienced a similar loss.

Allow Yourself to Feel: It's okay to experience a mix of emotions – sorrow, anger, relief, guilt. Your feelings are valid, and it's important to allow yourself to feel them.

Remember, there is no standard manual for navigating grief during these times. Each person's journey is unique, as is each person's grief. Your feelings might fluctuate from one moment to the next, and that's okay. What's important is to take care of yourself, to respect your feelings, and to find your way of remembering and honoring your loved one.

Strategies for Managing Grief During Special Occasions

Special occasions have a peculiar way of magnifying our emotions, especially when dealing with the loss of a beloved child. The laughter and joy around you can feel out of place, and your heart may feel heavy with the weight of their absence. It is during these times that grief can sneak up on you, often with an intensity that you may not have anticipated.

On his first birthday following his departure from us, the sense of grief we felt was incredibly profound, almost palpable. He had always wanted to spend his birthday in Las Vegas, a wish we decided to fulfill in his memory. In honor of his cherished dream, my youngest son, daughter, and I made the journey to Las Vegas, symbolically bringing him along with us. We chose to be in the city he could not be in physically, embracing the bittersweet reality.

During the poignant darkness of the night, we lit candles, their gentle glow a tribute to his vibrant spirit. We sat in silence, each lost in our thoughts, collectively longing for his presence. In navigating our grief, this personal tradition provided a sense of comfort and a coping strategy for dealing with the painful absence on special occasions. It's my hope that sharing our experience may serve as a guide for others traversing a similar path of loss and remembrance.

Anticipate the Pain: Recognize that these days will be difficult, and that's okay. There is no right or wrong way to feel. Anticipating the pain can allow you to create a plan for how you want to spend the day, whether that involves being surrounded by loved ones, spending time alone, or participating in an activity that brings you comfort.

Create a Ritual: Developing a ritual can provide a sense of control over an otherwise overwhelming day. This can be as simple as visiting your child's grave, releasing balloons with messages to them, or spending the day doing something they loved. It's a way of honoring their memory while also managing your grief.

Take Care of Your Physical Health: Grief can often manifest in physical ways, so it's essential to look after your health. Try to get enough sleep, eat nutritious food, and engage in physical activity. This can help you have the strength to cope with your emotions.

Seek Support: Reach out to those who understand and support you. Share your feelings, your fears, your memories. Sometimes, just having someone listen can provide immense relief.

Allow for Change: Over time, the intensity of your grief may change, and so too may the way you choose to commemorate your child on these special days. Allow for this change. What suits you one year may not the next, and that is perfectly fine.

The journey through grief is one that changes and evolves, just as our lives do. As such, it is essential to remain open and adaptable, especially during special occasions. The strategies I found most beneficial might evolve for you, but these additional points might provide a measure of comfort. Express Your Feelings: There's no need to keep your emotions bottled up. It's alright to cry, to be angry, or even to laugh. Our feelings are a testament to the love we had for our children and expressing them can be a part of the healing process.

Remember the Happy Moments: It might be painful to revisit memories, but it can also be therapeutic. Don't be afraid to remember the happy times, to share funny anecdotes, or to talk about your child. The joy they brought into our lives remains a part of us and remembering it can bring a measure of solace.

Nurture Your Spirit: Whether through prayer, meditation, yoga, or simply sitting in a garden, nurturing your spirit can provide an outlet for your grief. Find a peaceful activity that allows you to feel connected to your child and find some tranquility amidst the storm of emotions.

Reach out to Others: Connecting with other parents who have experienced a similar loss can be immensely comforting. They can offer understanding, empathy, and advice that comes from a place of shared experience. Many communities and online platforms offer support groups for bereaved parents, which can be an invaluable resource.

Do Something Meaningful: Many find comfort in doing something that commemorates their child's life, like planting a tree, starting a scholarship fund in their name, or volunteering at a charity they cared about. It's a way of channeling your grief into something positive and perpetuating the love and influence of your child.

Chapter 9: Handling Grief Triggers

The landscape of grief is pockmarked with triggers, unexpected moments or instances that may suddenly reignite your pain. These triggers, as unique and personal as the love you shared with your child, can turn a routine day into an emotional maelstrom. The scent of their favorite dish cooking, a song on the radio, or a glimpse of a child with the same hair color - any of these things and a thousand more can be a grief trigger. Yet, as disheartening as they are, they also offer a path to understanding and navigating your grief more effectively.

In this chapter, we will venture into the labyrinth of grief triggers. Understanding their nature, recognizing their impact, and learning how to manage them can help demystify the grieving process and make it feel less like an unpredictable rollercoaster. They are not the enemy, but signposts that mark your personal journey of healing. By identifying your personal triggers, developing coping strategies, and knowing when to seek help, you can gradually transform these instances of pain into opportunities for emotional resilience and growth.

Identifying Your Personal Triggers

The kaleidoscope of grief, with its manifold colors and shifting patterns, is replete with triggers – those emotional tripwires that send a sharp surge of sorrow coursing through you. Identifying these triggers is an essential step in your journey through grief. Each of us has unique triggers, personalized reminders of our loss, which can spring upon us in the most unexpected of moments. But remember, while these may appear like foes lurking in the shadows, they are in truth signals from our hearts, reminding us of our profound love for the one we lost.

Identifying personal triggers requires a kind of self-awareness that might feel overwhelming at times. You may find that certain sounds, smells, places, dates, or even phrases resonate with your sorrow. These might be as simple as the smell of a certain brand of soap your child used, the sound of a video game they loved, or the sight of their favorite meal. There is no rhyme or reason to these triggers, they are as unique and multifaceted as the person you loved.

It's helpful to keep a grief journal, a sacred space where you can record these triggers as they occur. It's not a task to fear but a form of acceptance and acknowledgment. Jot down what caused the rush of grief, how you felt, and any thoughts or memories associated with it. This process isn't designed to cause pain, but to offer a way to express your feelings, to face your grief head-on rather than avoiding it.

This endeavor will be demanding, there's no denying it. Yet, in time, you may find that these entries, these triggers, begin to form a poignant mosaic of the relationship you had with your child. You will begin to see not just the form of your grief, but also the shape of your love, etched in every reaction, every memory, every tear. In a paradoxical way, the very triggers that invoke pain are also bridges to the love you shared, and in time, to healing. But remember, you need not undertake this task alone. It's perfectly fine to reach out for support, from a trusted friend, a family member, or a professional counselor as you navigate this part of your journey.

In some cases, triggers may become less frequent or less intense, transforming into bittersweet reminders rather than sources of fresh anguish. Over time, you might find that the same song that once sent you spiraling into despair now brings a tearful smile as it reminds you of a happy memory with your child.

Similarly, visiting a place you once frequented together might shift from a painful reminder of their absence to a space where you can feel their lingering presence. Remember, it's okay to feel both joy and sorrow in these moments; it's a testament to the intricate tapestry of human emotions and the complexity of love and loss.

On the flip side, you might also find new triggers cropping up months or even years down the line. A random line in a book, a scene from a movie, or a significant life event might stir up emotions you thought you'd mastered. Don't be disheartened if this happens. Grief isn't a straight-line journey; it meanders and circles back, and that's perfectly normal.

Eventually, your relationship with your triggers will become a barometer for your grief journey, revealing the layers of your healing process. Recognizing and documenting these changes can serve as an affirmation of your resilience and the progress you've made, however incremental it may seem. At the end of the day, remember that there is no "right" way to handle triggers. The important thing is that you're taking the time and space to understand them, to sit with them, and to work through them in a way that feels right to you. This process is a part of your unique journey toward healing and self-compassion.

Developing Strategies for Coping with Triggers

Navigating the turbulent seas of grief, I found myself often caught in the undertow of unexpected triggers. But as painful as they were, these triggers also became my guideposts, signaling to me areas where I still needed to heal. As I ventured deeper into my grief journey, I began to understand that these triggers could be managed, that I could learn to live with them and use them as steppingstones on my path to healing.

Developing strategies for coping with grief triggers is as unique as our grief journey itself. For me, the process began with acceptance – acknowledging the presence of these triggers and the pain they bring, instead of attempting to suppress or avoid them. Embracing their existence is the first step towards learning how to cope.

The next step was learning to anticipate them, especially around certain dates, places, or events. This awareness allowed me to prepare myself emotionally, building resilience against the upcoming tide of grief. Preparation may take the form of personal rituals, setting aside quiet moments for reflection, or seeking the presence of a trusted loved one to lend support.

Remember, it's perfectly okay to set boundaries to protect yourself. If certain people, situations, or conversations tend to trigger your grief, it's acceptable to avoid them or to express your needs clearly. For example, if a particular conversation topic is likely to upset you, it's okay to ask the other person to steer clear of it.

At times, though, you might find it beneficial to lean into your triggers, to let them open the doorway to processing your grief. Writing has been one of my preferred methods for doing this. Pouring my thoughts and feelings into a journal provided a safe space to face these triggers and to navigate the emotions they stirred up.

I also learned the power of self-care in managing triggers. This could be anything from ensuring a good night's sleep, eating healthy food, taking a walk-in nature, or indulging in a favorite hobby. The act of taking care of myself physically helped to build resilience against the emotional impact of triggers. But remember, these are strategies that have helped me, and they may or may not resonate with you.

The coping mechanisms you develop will be as unique as your own journey of grief, reflecting your personal needs and preferences. The key is to experiment and find what works best for you, and to remember that what works may change as you move through different stages of your grief journey.

Yes, the path to managing grief triggers is filled with trial and error, but each step, each stumble, and each victory taught me more about my resilience and my capacity for healing. During one of my lowest moments, I found comfort in the most unexpected place - music. Songs that once filled me with pain now served as vessels of solace and understanding. I created playlists that embodied my emotions and allowed myself the freedom to dance, to cry, or to simply sit in silence as the music filled the room. Music became a therapeutic outlet for me, a way to express the sorrow that often felt too immense to put into words.

Yet, it's important to remember that it's perfectly okay to not have it all figured out. There are days when the triggers would hit out of the blue, catching me off guard, and I would feel myself spiraling. On these days, I learned to practice forgiveness - towards myself. I would remind myself that healing is not linear, that it's okay to have bad days, and that every moment of pain was a step towards healing.

Breathing exercises became my solace during such overwhelming moments. The simple act of closing my eyes, taking deep breaths, and centering myself helped me regain my composure. Just focusing on the rise and fall of my chest provided a sense of calm amidst the storm of my emotions. This might seem trivial, but these small islands of tranquility amid the tumultuous sea of grief were vital to my journey.

There were moments when the external world felt overwhelmingly burdensome, and in such times, I found solace not just in the embrace of nature, but also in spending quality time with my four Huskies. Whether it was a tranquil walk in the park, a moment of solitude on a beach, or simply sitting in my backyard watching the birds and interacting with my dogs, these instances provided me with a profound sense of calm. They served as subtle reminders of the larger cycle of life and death, growth and withering, embodying the enduring beauty of existence. Again, these are my experiences, my strategies. Yours might be entirely different. The important thing is to keep exploring, to keep trying, until you find what works for you.

Remember, there is no right or wrong way to grieve, and there is no right or wrong way to cope with grief triggers. We each have our own paths to walk, our own healing journeys to undertake. And while the path may seem dark now, know that with time, patience, and self-love, you will find your way towards healing.

Seeking Help When Needed

There are times in our journey through grief when the sorrow is too profound, the triggers too potent, the sense of loneliness too overwhelming. At such times, reaching out for help isn't just advisable, it's crucial. During these low points of my grief journey, I sought out counseling and therapy.

Navigating the healing path on your own can be taxing and often counterproductive. Despite the strength you may possess, grief has a way of depleting your emotional reserves and clouding your ability to cope effectively. There's no shame in reaching out to a grief counselor or a mental health professional for assistance. In fact, I found my therapy sessions to be incredibly transformative. My therapist provided me with a safe space to express my grief, my guilt, my anger, and my fears. She equipped me with strategies and techniques to handle my grief triggers and manage my anxiety.

In addition to therapy, I also sought solace in support groups. These were gatherings, either online or in person, of people who had experienced similar losses. There was comfort in the shared silence, in the mutual understanding that words often failed to capture our collective heartache. Hearing their stories, their coping mechanisms, their small victories and crushing setbacks, gave me a sense of camaraderie. It also served as a reminder that I was not alone in my pain.

If you are hesitant to reach out to professionals, talking to a trusted friend or family member can also provide relief. It was difficult for me initially to share my raw grief with others, fearing I might burden them. But I realized, by keeping my pain inside, I was only exacerbating my feelings of isolation and loneliness. The people who care about you want to support you, even if they might not understand your pain entirely. In my journey, I have learned that asking for help is not a sign of weakness, but a testament to my strength. It takes courage to face your pain, to admit that you are struggling, and to reach out for support. Remember, it is okay to lean on others. It is okay to seek professional help. We are not meant to face this journey alone, and there is help available when we are ready to accept it. Don't hesitate to reach out, to share, to seek support. You are not alone.

Chapter 10: Healing Through Creative Expression

Grief, like an ocean, is an expanse so vast and deep that words often fall short in expressing its magnitude. And yet, it is within this vastness that we often find the most poignant form of expression - creativity. This chapter delves into the healing power of creative expression, exploring how the arts can offer a comforting outlet for the emotions we grapple with, providing a tangible form to our intangible grief.

From the age-old traditions of memorial art and music to the simple act of journaling, creative outlets offer a sanctuary, a space where we can meet our grief, interact with it, and even transform it. Through creativity, we not only externalize our feelings but also engage with them on a deeper, more intimate level. This process isn't about crafting perfect art, but about nurturing an honest and brave conversation with our grief - a dialogue that promotes understanding, acceptance, and healing. So, let's embark on this journey of creative exploration, traversing through writing, art, music, and movement, to discover how these expressions can weave a healing balm for our shattered hearts.

Writing and Journaling

In the weeks and months following my son's passing, words became my solace. There was something comforting about the crisp, blank pages of my journal, like a silent companion ready to listen without judgment. As a mother who has experienced the unimaginable loss of a child, I found writing and journaling to be an avenue to pour my deepest emotions, a vessel to carry my most profound sorrow and a mirror to reflect my path towards healing.

It began as a raw outpouring, each word etched with tears, laden with the weight of loss. My pen danced to the rhythm of my broken heart, spelling out the anguish and despair that coursed through my veins. I wrote about the moment I heard the news, the crushing wave of sorrow, and the unbearable silence that followed. I wrote about the sleepless nights, the echoing emptiness of an empty house, my son's empty chair at the dinner table and the crippling loneliness that had become my shadow. It was heart-wrenching, but it was necessary.

But my journal was more than just a collection of my sorrows; it also held the essence of my love for my son. I wrote about his laughter, the way his eyes twinkled when he was excited, and how his presence filled a room. I wrote about our shared moments, the lessons he taught me, and how he changed my life for the better. Amid the tears, I found myself smiling, even laughing, as memories of him filled the pages. In grief, I had forgotten that it was possible, but through my words, I was reminded that joy and sorrow could coexist, that my love for him was not only etched in my loss but also in the beautiful moments we shared.

Writing and journaling are powerful tools in navigating the grief journey. Here are some ways they can help:

Emotional Release: Writing allows for the expression of deep emotions that might be difficult to articulate in conversation. It can provide an unfiltered outlet for your pain, fear, guilt, or anger, which can be incredibly cathartic.

Reflection and Understanding: By putting your feelings into words, you can gain a clearer understanding of your emotions and thoughts. This self-reflection can be crucial in processing your grief and in identifying any troubling thoughts or patterns that may require attention.

Documentation of Healing: Your journal can serve as a tangible documentation of your healing journey. Looking back, you can see how far you've come, the shifts in your emotions, the moments of understanding, and the first sparks of hope.

Connection with Your Lost Child: Writing about your child, their life, and your memories of them can help maintain a sense of connection. It can be a space to 'speak' to them, to remember, to celebrate, and to mourn.

I remember the day I realized that my journal had become a sacred space, a conduit between me and my son, a bridge between my love and my loss. And as I continued to write, I discovered that my words were not only stitching together the fragments of my broken heart but also laying down the steppingstones on my path to healing.

Art and Creative Outlets

My son had an uncanny ability to find joy in the simplest of things. He could spend hours in the backyard, lost in his world of wonder, sketching everything from the vivid daisies to the old, gnarled oak tree. When he died, he left a void that was both immense and intimate, a space that words seemed inadequate to fill. So, I turned to art, a language we both shared, to express the inexpressible.

I began to sketch, clumsy at first, my hands unsteady and uncertain. But as I allowed my emotions to guide my strokes, I found my heart pouring itself onto the canvas. My grief took form in bold, dark lines, my love in delicate strokes of vibrant colors, and my longing in the empty spaces that echoed my loss. I sketched my son, his laughter, his innocence, his adventurous spirit, bringing him alive on the canvas. It was a profound experience, one that allowed me to feel a sense of connection, of closeness with him.

Art became more than a creative outlet; it became a pathway to my healing. Each stroke, each blend of color, each creation was a step towards acknowledging my pain, understanding it, and ultimately transforming it. Art, in its many forms, can serve as a cathartic release, a safe space to express your grief, and an opportunity to honor your child in a unique and personal way.

Here are some ways art and creative outlets can be therapeutic:

Visual Expression: Grief is a complex emotion, sometimes too overwhelming for words. Art allows you to communicate your feelings visually, capturing the nuances of your emotions in a way that words might not.

Connection to Your Child: Creating art that reflects your child's personality, passions, or shared memories can help you feel a sense of connection to them. It can be a meaningful tribute to their life.

Mindfulness and Focus: The process of creating art requires focus and presence, which can provide a much-needed respite from your grief. It encourages mindfulness, helping you stay connected to the present moment.

Emotional Release: Just like writing, art can serve as a channel for emotional release. It's a safe space to express your pain, fear, confusion, or even anger.

Healing and Transformation: Art can be a transformative process. As you express your grief through your creations, you may find it evolves over time, mirroring your healing journey.

When I look at the sketches I created in those early days of grief, I see not only my sorrow but also my resilience. I see a mother who refused to let her grief consume her, who found a way to express her loss and honor her son. Art, in its boundless forms, held my hand through my darkest days, offering a beacon of hope in the swirling storm of grief. It reminded me that even in loss, beauty persists, and even in death, love endures.

As I became more comfortable with my sketchbook, I began to explore other artistic mediums. I started painting, experimenting with the burst of colors and the fluidity of the brush strokes. Each hue seemed to echo a different emotion, a different memory of my son. The gentle blues spoke of the brilliance of his eyes, the fiery reds of his fierce loyalty to his family and friends, the soft greens reminded me of all the money he wanted to make. The canvas became a testament of my love for him, a silent, vibrant elegy to his life.

Sculpting became another avenue of expression for me. The tangible nature of clay, its flexibility, and the power to mold it into form was a potent reminder of my resilience. As I shaped and reshaped the clay, it was as if I was learning to reshape my life around the void left by my son's passing. It was a silent declaration that while my grief was a part of me, it wouldn't define me.

Photography, too, held its unique healing power. Through the lens, I could capture the world as my son might have seen it - full of wonder, beauty, and endless possibilities. It made me feel closer to him, sharing the same vision, if only for a fleeting moment.

Here are some other creative outlets that can be helpful in your healing journey:

Collage Art: Collecting images, colors, textures that resonate with your emotions and composing them into a collage can be therapeutic. It can be a mood board of your feelings or a tribute to your child's life.

Star Gazing: Using a telescope to observe the cosmos can create a unique sense of connection with your departed loved one. The act of peering into the infinite depths of space offers a tranquil setting to reflect and find solace in your grief. Observing the cosmos allows you to contemplate life from a wider perspective and find peace in the majestic beauty of the universe.

Craft: Creating something for or about your child, like a scrapbook or a memory box, can be a comforting project. It allows you to engage with your memories in a tangible way.

Gardening: The act of nurturing life, witnessing growth and transformations can be a metaphor for your healing journey. Planting a memorial garden or a tree in memory of your child connects you with nature, offering peace and tranquility.

I discovered that art in its varied forms became a language that gave voice to my silence, a balm that soothed my aching heart, and a bridge that connected me to my son. It was a space where I could be honest, vulnerable, and brave. A space where I could grieve and heal at the same time. It taught me that creativity and grief could coexist, each nurturing the other, ultimately leading to a journey of healing and self-discovery.

Music and Movement

For as long as I can remember, my son had a rhythm in his soul. His laughter was a melody that echoed throughout our home, his spirit a dance that radiated joy. The memory of his love for music became my companion in the solitude of grief. It was a link to him, a thread of connection that I held onto dearly. A song he loved, a tune he hummed, the beats he tapped on the kitchen table; they were all part of our shared soundtrack. In my darkest hours, I found solace in this symphony of memories.

I first turned to music as a source of comfort, a gentle refuge where I could feel his presence. Listening to his favorite songs was like having a part of him with me. The lyrics held new meanings, the melodies echoed his laughter, his dreams, his essence. Music became a language through which I could express my grief, my longing, my love.

And then, I discovered the healing power of creating music. I started learning the piano, a dream my son and I had often talked about. My fingers were clumsy at first, faltering over the keys. But with each note, each chord, each melody, I felt a sense of connection with him.

It was as if, through the music, I could convey the words left unsaid, the emotions too profound to articulate. Music became an outlet for my grief, a medium through which I could honor my son's memory.

Here are some ways in which music and movement can aid in your healing journey:

Listening to Music: Music has the power to soothe, comfort, and heal. Listening to your child's favorite songs, or songs that remind you of them, can help you feel connected to them.

Creating Music: Learning an instrument, singing, or writing songs can be therapeutic. It allows you to express your emotions and create something beautiful in their memory.

Movement and Dance: Dance is a form of expression that engages both the body and the soul. It allows you to physically express your grief and can be a source of catharsis.

Music Therapy: Professional music therapists can guide you through the process of using music to express and understand your emotions. It can be a safe space to explore your grief and find healing.

In my journey of grief, I also found solace in movement. It began with long walks in the park, where I could feel the wind whispering tales of my son. The rustling leaves seemed to echo his laughter, the blooming flowers his radiant smile. With each step, I felt a sense of release, as if I was leaving behind a tiny fragment of my sorrow with the receding path.

Gradually, I found myself drawn to dance, a testament to my son's vibrant spirit. In the solitude of my living room, I let the music guide my movements. Some days, my dance was a mirror of my sorrow, slow and heavy. Other days, it was a celebration of my son's life, vibrant and full of energy. But always, it was a reflection of my love for him, an ode to our shared moments.

Through music and movement, I found a rhythm in my grief. It became a dance of love, sorrow, and healing, a symphony of my journey as a bereaved mother. And in this dance, I found not only solace but also a sense of connection to my son, a rhythm that beats in synchrony with my heart, a song that carries his memory into every tomorrow.

Chapter 11: Connecting with Others Who Have Experienced Loss

The pain of losing a child creates a divide, a chasm between the life you once lived and the world you now inhabit. This new world can feel isolating and daunting, as though you are lost in a wilderness with no trail to guide you. Yet, you are not alone. Others, too, have traveled this difficult terrain, and their experiences, wisdom, and empathy can serve as lighthouses in your darkest nights.

Reaching out to others who have faced similar losses may feel daunting at first, but these connections can prove incredibly comforting and enlightening. It is a community no one wishes to belong to, but it is one that understands your anguish as few can.

In this chapter, we will explore the importance of finding shared experiences, building a support network, and learning from the grief journeys of others. How do you find these connections? How can they support you through your grief journey, and how can you, in turn, support others? These are the questions we will be delving into, with the goal of helping you find companionship, understanding, and solace on your own journey through loss.

Finding Shared Experiences and Understanding

It was a support group for grieving parents that first introduced me to the idea of shared experiences and understanding. I still remember the profound impact of those first meetings, stepping into a room filled with individuals who had also experienced the unimaginable loss of a child. While I had been cocooned in my sorrow, these meetings awakened in me the realization that I was not alone in my grief. There was a kind of silent understanding that permeated the room, an unspoken acknowledgment that everyone there was carrying the same heavy burden.

Though our stories were different, the pain was universally recognizable. Each of us had been thrown into a storm of grief and were trying to make sense of a world that had suddenly turned unrecognizable. In the midst of our shared struggle, there was a deep sense of comfort, almost relief. Being seen, truly seen, in my grief, without judgment, without the need for explanation, was a healing experience in itself. These connections became a lifeline, a beacon of light in my darkest hours.

From a broader perspective, shared experiences in loss can serve as a powerful reminder that grief, in all its painful reality, is part of the universal human experience. It's not just about the commiseration of shared pain, but also about the understanding that each of us copes with grief in our own way. Every grief journey is unique, but the feelings of loss, the questions we grapple with, the process of trying to find meaning in the aftermath – these are shared experiences. By seeking out and acknowledging these shared experiences, we begin to break down the walls of isolation that grief often builds.

Consider, as you navigate your own path of grief:

- Attending support group meetings, either in-person or virtually. Hearing others' stories and sharing your own can provide a deep sense of understanding and solidarity.

- Seeking out online forums, social media groups, or websites dedicated to the experience of child loss. While the virtual world can never replace in-person connections, it can provide a valuable space for shared experiences and understanding.

- Reading memoirs or books about grief and loss. While every story is unique, you may find echoes of your own experiences and emotions in the words of others.

As you journey through your grief, remember, there's no 'right' way to grieve, and it's okay to seek out connections when you feel ready. There's strength in shared experiences, and in the understanding and empathy that come with them. The connection with others can act as a bridge over the turbulent waters of grief, offering solace, understanding, and a sense of community. It's about finding a place where your grief is understood, validated, and respected – a place where you can truly be seen.

The truth is, grief can feel like an insurmountable wall, isolating us from the rest of the world. Yet, it's this very wall that can crumble when we allow ourselves to connect with others who've been through a similar experience. Over time, as I attended more support group sessions, I began to notice subtle changes in the way I carried my grief. It didn't become less painful, but it did become less lonely. I felt less like a solitary figure in an endless sea of pain and more like a member of a compassionate, understanding community.

Sharing my story also gave me a sense of agency over my grief. I was no longer just the woman who lost her child; I was a woman with a story to tell, a woman with experiences that could perhaps help others in their moments of pain. Sharing my grief journey became a form of healing, a way to give purpose to my pain. And in the compassionate faces of those around me, I saw my own grief reflected, understood, and gently held.

In the wider context, it's important to remember that finding shared experiences is not about comparing tragedies or measuring grief. It's about witnessing and honoring each other's pain. It's about acknowledging that while grief is a path we walk alone, we don't have to be lonely.

Here are a few thoughts to remember:

It's okay if you're not ready to share your own story. Just listening can be a healing experience. It can make you feel seen, even if you're not yet ready to step into the light.

It's alright to take a step back if you find the shared experiences overwhelming. Grief is a personal journey, and it's essential to take care of your emotional wellbeing.

Remember, shared experiences can be found in unexpected places. A heartfelt conversation with a friend who has experienced a different kind of loss can still bring comfort and understanding.

Engaging with shared experiences can be a courageous step towards healing. You may find understanding and comfort in shared stories, shared tears, and shared silence. And perhaps, in the process, you may discover that the love you have for your lost child can exist alongside hope, compassion, and a newfound resilience. Embrace the journey and remember you are not alone.

Building a Support Network

Life after loss is like trying to navigate a labyrinth in the dark. It's easy to feel lost, disoriented, even hopeless. But one thing I've learned on my journey is that you don't have to walk this path alone. Building a support network became my torchlight, illuminating my path and making the journey a little less daunting.

In the early days, I leaned heavily on my immediate family. My daughter, son, and stepson were my pillars of strength, their shared pain a bitter but solid bond that kept us together. But I also understood they were grappling with their own grief. I realized that while our pain was shared, our healing journeys would be individual and unique.

It was then that I began to reach out. I joined grief support groups, both in-person and online. What I found in those spaces was a lifeline - a community of people who understood the depth of my pain. They didn't shy away from my tears; they didn't feel uncomfortable with my sorrow. Instead, they met me with empathy, understanding, and the knowledge that my pain, while unique, was not solitary. I felt seen, heard, and held.

However, it's important to understand that a support network isn't built overnight:

Start small. It could be just one friend or a family member who is comfortable with your grief and willing to listen without judgment.

Consider professional help. Therapists and counselors trained in grief support can provide valuable tools to navigate your journey of loss.

Reach out to support groups. They offer a safe space to share your feelings with those who've been where you are.

Don't feel rushed to build your network. Everyone's pace is different, and it's crucial to do what feels right for you.

As my support network grew, so did my ability to carry my grief. It was no longer a solitary burden, but one shared by many hands. And while the absence of my son didn't diminish, my ability to live with that absence grew. Building my support network wasn't about erasing my pain; it was about learning to live a meaningful life alongside it.

Building a support network wasn't just about the people I met in support groups or therapy sessions. I found comfort in unexpected places too. Friends from my son's life reached out, and their shared stories and memories brought me solace. While their presence reminded me of the magnitude of my loss, it also reminded me of the joy and love my son had brought into so many lives. Sharing those memories became an important part of my healing journey.

As a single mother, I also had to confront the challenge of being the primary source of support for my other children while simultaneously grieving. It was during those times that I truly appreciated the value of my extended family and community. They stepped in when I was overwhelmed, providing a comforting presence for my younger son, daughter and stepson. Their involvement wasn't just about providing emotional support but also about the practical aspects of everyday life that were often overlooked in the throes of grief.

Be open to support from unexpected sources. It could be a friend from the past, a distant relative, or a neighbor.
Reach out to those who knew your loved one. Their shared memories can offer a different kind of solace.

Acknowledge and accept help with practical matters. Sometimes, a home-cooked meal or someone to run errands can be a huge relief.

Remember that it's okay to step back when needed. Your emotional well-being is paramount.

Building a support network is a journey, a journey of connection and mutual understanding. It taught me that grief, as isolating as it feels, can also connect us in profound and meaningful ways. It's through sharing our stories, our pain, and our resilience that we find strength, not just in ourselves, but also in the shared experiences of those around us.

Learning from the Grief Journeys of Others

As a mother who has lost a child, one of the most consoling aspects of my grief journey has been learning from the experiences of others. There is a certain comfort in knowing that others have walked this path and survived, that they too have felt this pain and somehow managed to keep going.

I remember one of the first meetings at the support group. It was there I met Wendy, a woman who had lost her daughter seven years prior. Wendy had a quiet strength about her. She was a beacon of hope in that room. What struck me about her was not just her survival, but her ability to smile, to find joy in life again despite the gaping hole in her heart.

Wendy shared stories of her own journey, the peaks and valleys of her grief, the strategies that had helped her to cope, and the ways she honored the memory of her daughter. She spoke of the rough days when getting out of bed felt like climbing Everest and of the days when she could laugh and reminisce without breaking down.

From Wendy and others, I learned that grief is a lifelong companion. It changes shape and form, it retreats and resurfaces, but it never truly leaves. But alongside it, joy, love, and life continue. They shared their stories of moving forward, not as individuals who had returned to their old selves, but as those who had been transformed by their loss, carrying it with them into their new selves.

- Every grief journey is unique, yet there is comfort in shared experiences.
- Learning from others does not mean comparing your grief. It is about understanding the multitude of ways in which people cope.
- Take inspiration from those further along their grief journey but remember that it's okay if your path looks different.
- You are not alone. There is a community of individuals who have walked and are walking this path. Draw strength from this shared experience.

In the end, listening to the grief journeys of others was about more than seeking comfort or trying to make sense of my feelings. It was a way of understanding the varied tapestry of human resilience and compassion. And in doing so, I found reassurance and strength, the assurance that as isolating as grief could be, there was a community out there who understood, who cared, and who were travelling the same rugged path.

Thank you, Dr. Wendy!

Chapter 12: Nurturing Your Mental Health

Experiencing the loss of a child is a profound encounter that engulfs you entirely, leaving you feeling completely numb. This all-consuming tragedy impacts every facet of your existence, particularly your mental health. This chapter is dedicated to acknowledging the importance of mental health during the grief journey and providing guidance on how to nurture it. While it is natural and expected to feel an overwhelming sadness and a multitude of other emotions following such a monumental loss, it's critical to discern between the normal process of grieving and signs that you may need additional help.

It's important to remember that it's okay not to be okay. You don't need to put on a brave face or hide your emotions. This journey is not about 'getting over' your grief but learning how to live with it. It's about finding ways to honor your child's memory, while also taking care of yourself.

In this chapter, we'll explore how to recognize and address signs of depression and anxiety, and the importance of seeking professional help when needed. This is not a journey you have to make alone, and seeking help is not a sign of weakness but a testament to your strength and love for your child.

Recognizing and Addressing Signs of Depression

In the aftermath of my son's death, the world felt colorless, as if draped in a permanent veil of gray. I found myself swimming in a sea of sorrow, waves of grief crashing over me relentlessly. Some days, getting out of bed felt like a Herculean task. I lost interest in activities I once enjoyed. I felt a constant sense of fatigue, even though I wasn't engaging in any physically strenuous activity. The simplest tasks seemed overwhelming. I noticed that my appetite waned, and so did my sleep. On the days I could sleep, I woke up still feeling tired, as if sleep had forgotten how to be restful. I also grappled with feelings of worthlessness and guilt, despite knowing that what had happened was beyond my control.

I didn't realize it then, but these were signs of depression. It's important to differentiate between the normal grieving process and clinical depression. While grief can incorporate many of the symptoms of depression, such as intense sadness, insomnia, and lack of appetite, it differs in a few key aspects.

Grief, although painful, usually decreases in intensity over time and occurs in waves, often triggered by thoughts or reminders of the deceased. Depression, on the other hand, is persistent. The feelings of emptiness and despair are constant and can interfere with your ability to function.

Here are some signs of depression to watch out for:

- Persistent feelings of sadness, emptiness, or hopelessness
- Loss of interest or pleasure in activities once enjoyed
- Significant weight loss or gain, or a decrease or increase in appetite
- Difficulty sleeping or oversleeping
- Constant fatigue or loss of energy
- Feelings of worthlessness, or excessive or inappropriate guilt
- Difficulty thinking, concentrating, or making decisions
- Recurrent thoughts of death or suicide.

If you identify with several of the above symptoms, and they've persisted for at least two weeks, it might be time to seek professional help. Understand that there's no shame in reaching out. I eventually sought help from a mental health professional, a decision that played a crucial role in my healing journey.

The depression I felt was not a sign of weakness, but a reflection of the deep love I had for my son and the immense loss I had suffered. It was a testament to my humanity, and treating it was a crucial step towards healing.

Anxiety and Grief

Alongside the crushing sadness that came with my son's death, I found an unexpected companion - anxiety. It lurked in the quiet moments, whispering fears and uncertainties that left me restless. Every unexpected bark of the dogs sent a wave of panic through me, causing my heart to race. I found myself constantly worrying about my other children, consumed by a fear of losing them too. Nights were especially challenging. Sleep was elusive, and when it did come, it was often punctuated by intense, realistic nightmares.

Anxiety, I soon learned, is a common companion to grief. The world, once familiar, suddenly feels uncertain and menacing. Your sense of safety is shattered. You've experienced firsthand how precarious life can be, and it's only natural to fear further loss.

Common signs of anxiety can include:

- Excessive worry or fear
- Feeling constantly "on edge" or restless
- Racing thoughts or uncontrollable over-thinking
- Difficulties concentrating or mind going blank
- Irritability, which may be evident to others
- Muscle tension or discomfort
- Difficulty falling asleep, staying asleep, or restless and unsatisfying sleep
- Increased heart rate or palpitations

Again, it's crucial to understand that experiencing anxiety does not mean you are failing in your grief journey. Grief and anxiety often walk hand in hand. It's your mind's way of grappling with a reality that feels unbearable. Recognizing the presence of anxiety, however, is the first step towards addressing it.

Seeking professional help was my lifeline. I started seeing a therapist who specialized in grief counseling. She guided me through relaxation techniques and grounding exercises that helped manage the anxiety. We talked about my fears, faced them head-on instead of letting them fester in the silence.

She reassured me that what I was feeling was a natural response to a traumatic event. There were days when the anxiety felt insurmountable, but each day, I took a small step forward. With time and therapy, I learned to navigate the anxious waters of grief, to find moments of calm amidst the turmoil. It wasn't easy, but it was necessary, not just for me, but for the well-being of my other children who needed me to be present.

Remember, it's okay to seek help. If you're experiencing symptoms of anxiety, reach out to a healthcare professional. There are numerous resources and therapies available that can provide significant relief. You don't have to face this alone. My healing journey began when I reached out for help. Your journey can begin there too.

Seeking Professional Help

When the magnitude of my loss seemed too overwhelming to bear, I found it difficult to voice my pain, even to those closest to me. I was drowning in a sea of grief, and it felt as if no one could understand the depth of my sorrow. I felt isolated in my grief, and this isolation added another layer of pain to my already aching heart.

It was during one of these bleak periods that I reached out for professional help. I had harbored reservations about seeing a therapist - the stigma, the fear of being judged, and to be honest, a part of me didn't believe that it could help. I wondered, how could talking to a stranger make any difference? But the grief was all-consuming, and I knew I needed help.

Seeing a therapist turned out to be one of the best decisions I could have made for my mental health. They provided me with a safe and non-judgmental space to express my grief. They didn't try to offer quick solutions or hollow condolences. Instead, they validated my feelings, normalized my pain, and provided me with coping strategies that I could use when the grief felt too intense.

In my sessions, I learned about the complexity of grief. I understood that it's okay not to move on from the loss, but rather to move forward with it. I learned how to incorporate my son's memory into my life in a way that didn't keep me stuck in the past, but rather allowed me to keep him alive in my heart as I moved forward.

Seeking professional help, like seeing a psychologist, psychiatrist, or a grief counselor, can provide a lifeline when you're navigating the choppy waters of grief. They are trained to understand the multifaceted nature of grief and can equip you with the tools you need to cope. They can help you recognize if your grief is leading to more serious mental health conditions, like depression or prolonged grief disorder, and can provide treatment or refer you to other professionals who can.

Remember, reaching out for help is not a sign of weakness, but a testament to your strength. You are trying to survive the unimaginable, and you don't have to do it alone. I'm grateful I took that step, as it played an instrumental role in my healing journey. My hope is that by sharing my story, you too will feel empowered to seek the help you need and know that it's okay to do so.

Thank you, Dr. Wendy.

Chapter 13: Rebuilding Your Life After Loss

There's a haunting beauty in the aftermath of a storm. The stillness that follows the tumultuous winds, the warmth of the sun seeping through the cloud-wrought sky, the world washed clean, ready to begin anew. This imagery, although an oversimplification, resonates with the process of grief. After traversing the challenging landscape of sorrow and despair, there comes a point where we begin to see the possibility of renewal, of reconstructing the fragments of our shattered world. This fourteenth chapter, "Rebuilding Your Life After Loss," is dedicated to this painstaking yet essential phase of the grief journey.

Grief, in all its harshness, has the capacity to reshape us, to usher in personal growth and transformation. It brings about a shift in our perspective, allowing us to view life through a different lens. It forces us to reevaluate our dreams, our goals, our very existence.

In this chapter, we will explore this process of embracing change, of nurturing new dreams, and of moving forward with love and gratitude. This chapter is a testament to the resilience of the human spirit and the remarkable capacity we hold for healing and growth even in the face of profound loss.

Embracing Personal Growth and Transformation

Grief changed me, like the earth is reshaped by the relentless beat of the waves. It didn't make me a different person, but rather a new version of myself, one sculpted by sorrow and loss. I had been a mother, a confidant. But after losing my child, I also became a survivor, a seeker of light in the deepest corners of sorrow. I had to learn to accept this transformation and see it not as a distortion, but an evolution of myself.

In the initial days, I spent hours looking in the mirror, searching for the woman I was before tragedy knocked on my door. The face staring back at me seemed like a stranger. My eyes, once alight with joy, now held an unfamiliar depth, a silent testament to the pain I carried. My laughter, when it did come, had a different timbre, a distinct note of melancholy that hadn't been there before. I had to come to terms with the fact that grief had left an indelible imprint on me.

But with time, I realized that this transformation was not a sentence to eternal misery, but a path towards personal growth. I began to see that the depth in my eyes was not just a reflection of my suffering but also a mark of resilience. The melancholy in my laughter was not an indicator of persistent sorrow, but a symbol of my ability to find joy, however fleeting, amidst pain.

Herein lies the crux of our journey. Embracing personal growth and transformation doesn't mean letting go of the person you were before. Rather, it's about accepting that you're becoming someone who can carry the weight of your loss while still moving forward. This isn't about forgetting or replacing your past self or the person you lost; it's about allowing grief to mold you into a person who can integrate the reality of your loss into your present and future.

- Reflect on your own transformation: Look back on how you've changed since your loss. Identify areas where you've grown, such as in your capacity to empathize with others or your resilience in the face of adversity.
- Be gentle with yourself: Remember that change is a gradual process. There will be setbacks, but these do not negate the growth you've already achieved.

- Seek professional help if needed: A mental health professional can guide you through this process of transformation, helping you to understand and accept your changes in a healthy way.

Embracing personal growth and transformation is about seeing the light within the darkness, about acknowledging the pain and choosing to grow through it. It's about taking the pieces of your shattered heart and rebuilding yourself with them, creating a mosaic of sorrow, resilience, and hope. It is from this place, this acceptance of transformation, that we can begin to navigate the next steps of our journey: establishing new goals and dreams.

Establishing New Goals and Dreams

In the aftermath of loss, the future can seem uncertain, even unfathomable. All the dreams I had nurtured for my son, all our shared aspirations for what lay ahead were abruptly severed. I was left bereft, not only of my beloved child but also of the future I had envisioned. It was as if a thick fog had descended, obscuring everything that lay ahead. But as I began to navigate my grief, I understood that finding my way through this fog was an integral part of my healing journey.

When someone you love becomes a memory, that memory becomes a treasure. And for me, the treasure was the dreams we had nurtured together. My son's dreams became part of my own. His aspirations, a compass guiding my path. His unfinished journey, a call to action. I realized that even though he was no longer physically present, I could continue to honor his memory by living out his dreams and infusing my own life with the passion he had for his.

This is not to say that it was easy. Redefining your future after a significant loss is a daunting task. But it's important to remember that setting new goals and dreams isn't about replacing the person you lost or forgetting about your shared dreams. It's about building on them, letting them evolve in a way that both honors the memory of your loved one and fosters your personal growth.

Here are some things that helped me in establishing new goals and dreams:

- Reflect on your loved one's aspirations: What were their passions, their dreams? How can you incorporate those into your own life in a meaningful way?

- Take small steps: Begin by setting small, achievable goals. This could be as simple as choosing to get out of bed each morning or taking up a hobby you've been interested in.
- Prioritize self-care: Set goals related to your own wellbeing. This could involve regular exercise, a balanced diet, mindfulness practices, or pursuing therapy.
- Don't rush: Grief has its own timetable. Give yourself permission to move at your own pace.

Establishing new goals and dreams after a loss may feel like you're walking a tightrope. Balancing the memory of your loved one with the need to move forward can be a delicate task. But remember, every step forward is a testament to your resilience and your capacity for love. As you navigate this new terrain, know that it's okay to change direction, to stumble, and to pause when needed. And through it all, you move forward with love, gratitude, and the resilience of your spirit.

As I continued this path of establishing new dreams and goals, I also learned to be patient with myself. There were days when it seemed like I was making progress, only to find myself back at square one the next day. But in time, I recognized that these were not steps backward but rather part of the ebb and flow of the grief process. Each day brought its own challenges, but also its own victories. Even on the hardest days, I found that there was always a glimmer of hope, a seed of a new dream waiting to be nurtured.

I began exploring interests that I had long neglected or never had the time for. I took painting classes, something that my son and I had often spoken about doing together. In the quiet hours spent in front of the canvas, I found a form of therapy. Each stroke of the brush felt like a way of reconnecting with my son, of bringing our shared dream to life. While it didn't alleviate the pain of loss, it brought a new sense of purpose and direction. It was as though each painting was a step toward a future where the pain of loss coexisted with the joy of memories.

Another part of establishing new goals and dreams involved finding ways to give back to the community. My son had always been passionate about helping others, so I started checking on his friends, carrying on his legacy of kindness and compassion. This not only gave me a new sense of purpose but also allowed me to connect with others who understood the language of loss. In their stories, I found echoes of my own experiences and, in turn, a sense of solidarity and understanding.

Gradually, as I nurtured these new dreams and goals, I found a new rhythm in life. I learned that moving forward wasn't about leaving my son behind, but about carrying him with me into this new future. His dreams became intertwined with my own, his memory the cornerstone of my new goals. As I built this new life, I realized that it wasn't just about surviving but about thriving. It was about honoring my son's memory, about building a life that he would be proud of.

Setting new goals and dreams after a loss is a deeply personal and transformative journey. It's about finding a way to carry your loved one's legacy forward while also rediscovering your own passions and purpose. It's about acknowledging the pain of your loss, but also recognizing your capacity for growth, love, and resilience. And most importantly, it's about understanding that even in the midst of grief, life can still hold the promise of new beginnings.

Moving Forward with Love and Gratitude

Every day that passes, each stride towards my altered objectives and aspirations, I find myself moving forward with an increasing awareness of love and gratitude. My path through grief and healing is not about negating the pain or wishing it away; instead, it's about recognizing this pain as an integral part of my life's narrative. I cherish the memories I have of my son, our shared love, and the insights I gained from our time together. I'm profoundly grateful for the time we were given, even though it feels like he was called home too soon. He may no longer be with me in physical form, yet he continues to play a significant role in my life, forever present in my heart and mind.

I began to find strength in gratitude. I was grateful for the time I had with my son, for the love we shared, and for the beautiful memories that I could hold onto. I was grateful for the lessons of love, compassion, and resilience that his life and death had taught me. I was grateful for the people who stood by me, for the bonds that were forged in the crucible of grief. And, perhaps most surprisingly, I was grateful for the journey of grief itself, for it had led me to a deeper understanding of myself and my place in the world.

Moving forward with love and gratitude also meant learning to let go of guilt and regret. It was about accepting that there were things beyond my control and learning to make peace with the unchangeable past. It was about forgiving myself for the things I couldn't change and focusing instead on the things I could – my response to grief, my path to healing, and my journey to a life that honored my son's memory.

In embracing gratitude, I also discovered the power of love. Love for my son, love for those around me, and, gradually, love for myself. This love wasn't just an emotion, it was an active choice - a choice to keep my son's memory alive, to continue loving him, and to extend that love to others who were also navigating their own paths of grief and healing.

Ultimately, rebuilding my life after loss was about integrating my grief into my new reality, about finding a way to honor my son's memory while also rediscovering joy and purpose. It was about embracing personal transformation, establishing new goals and dreams, and moving forward with love and gratitude. The journey was filled with pain, but also with profound moments of love, growth, and beauty. It was a testament to the resilience of the human spirit, a reminder that even in the face of profound loss, it is possible to rebuild and find meaning again.

Chapter 14: The Path to Healing

As we approach the end of this book, the end of this shared journey through my experience of profound loss, it is crucial to understand that no conclusion is in sight when it comes to grief. It is not a destination, but rather a path we tread, a part of our journey that molds us, changes us, and becomes a part of who we are. As such, it's not about seeking an end to grief but learning to honor it and weave it into the fabric of our lives.

In this final chapter, we will explore the acceptance of our grief journeys, our resilience, and the strength we find within ourselves. We'll speak of the hope that's nurtured, not just for a day or a month, but for a future that carries the imprints of loss and the strength born from it. This chapter is a homage to all that we have endured, the love we keep in our hearts, and the unending process of healing and growing that follows the loss of a child. So, let's step forward, honoring our unique journeys and cherishing the resilience and hope that guides us towards a future that can still hold joy, love, and life.

Honoring Your Grief Journey

Every grief journey is as unique as the individual who embarks on it, and as profound as the love they held for the person they lost. For me, losing my son was a pain that altered the very essence of my existence, every fiber of my being. It was a raw, consuming pain that seemed to eclipse all else. Yet, as time went on, I learned that this pain was not something to be shamed or shunned, but a testament to the deep love I held for my child.

In honoring our grief journeys, we must first accept that our grief is our own. It is as personal and individual as our fingerprints. There is no right or wrong way to grieve, no timeline that fits all, no feelings that are out of place. I've had days when the sadness was so overwhelming it felt like a physical weight, days when anger consumed me, and days when I've found myself smiling at a memory, only to feel guilty the next moment.

Yet, every step I took, every tear I shed, every moment I remembered my son, was a part of my grief journey. It was not just about the pain and loss, but also about the love and connection that death could not sever. It was about remembering my son, not just as someone I had lost, but as an integral part of my life, my identity, my story.

Honoring your grief journey means acknowledging every emotion, every struggle, every moment of despair, and every small victory. It means accepting that grief has changed you, and that is okay. It means recognizing that your journey might not look like anyone else's, and that's okay too. It means understanding that grief is not a sign of weakness, but a testament to your capacity to love and to endure, a testament of strength.

I remember, early in my grief, I would sometimes feel like I was 'not grieving right.' I would compare my grief to others', worry about 'moving on' too fast or too slow, about not feeling 'sad enough' or feeling 'too sad.' It took me time, patience, and self-compassion to understand that my grief journey was my own, that it was not bound by societal expectations or timelines. That it was okay to feel what I felt when I felt it.

Honoring my grief journey became about allowing myself to feel the pain, the loss, the love, and the connection. It was about creating space for my grief, not as a destructive force, but as a part of my love for my son, a part of my healing, a part of me. So, as we walk this path, let us remember to honor our individual grief journeys, for they are testaments of our love, our strength, and our resilience.

Embracing Resilience and Strength

The grieving process is not linear, and it's not predictable. It's a winding road, full of unexpected twists and turns, ups and downs, dark nights and bright dawns. But as I journeyed through my own grief, I realized something profound. I was more resilient than I ever knew. I was stronger than I had ever imagined. I had faced the worst that life could possibly throw at me, and I was still standing, still moving forward, still finding moments of joy amid the sorrow.

When we speak about resilience and strength, it's not about not feeling pain, or about bouncing back as if nothing has happened. Resilience is about feeling the pain, acknowledging it, living through it, and yet, being able to find a way forward. It's about learning to carry our grief, our love, and our loss, in a way that does not incapacitate us, but allows us to live, to grow, to hope.

Strength, too, is not about being unaffected or unbroken. It's about being broken and yet choosing to put ourselves back together, one piece at a time. It's about embracing our vulnerabilities, our pain, our sorrow, and yet, not letting them define us. It's about holding on to who we are, who we were, and who we can still become.

Throughout my grief journey, I had moments of despair and moments of determination, moments of weakness and moments of incredible strength. I cried, I mourned, I raged, I questioned, and I also hoped, loved, and dreamed. I realized that my resilience and my strength were not in spite of my grief, but because of it. It was my grief that showed me how strong I could be, how resilient I was.

Embracing resilience and strength is about recognizing our capacity to endure, to adapt, to grow. It's about acknowledging that we have faced the unimaginable and are still here, still trying, still hoping. It's about accepting that we can be both - broken and whole, grieving and joyful, lost and found.

The journey through grief is a testament to our resilience and strength. As we continue to navigate through our loss, as we continue to honor our loved ones and our grief, let's also honor our resilience and our strength. Let's remember that we have faced the worst and we are still here, still standing, still moving forward. And that, in itself, is an act of immense courage, resilience, and strength.

Nurturing Hope for the Future

Grief has a way of making the future seem unattainable, even undesirable. It shrouds the tomorrow in an impenetrable fog, leaving us stranded in our yesterdays. Yet, as we journey through our grief, slowly but surely, we begin to see a hint of tomorrow emerging. A tomorrow different from what we had envisioned, yes, but a tomorrow, nevertheless.

It starts with little moments, a faint flicker of hope, like the sun trying to break through a cloud-covered sky. You find yourself laughing at a silly joke, engrossed in a good book, or planning a meet-up with friends. It feels odd, surreal even, to experience these moments of normalcy amidst your grief. But these moments, fleeting as they are, hint at a profound truth. Life, with its inherent propensity for renewal, continues, even when we feel stuck in our grief.

Hope, I've learned, is not a destination, nor is it a state of perpetual happiness. It's a process, an act of faith, a quiet courage. It's choosing to believe in possibilities, even when reality seems devoid of them. It's about nurturing a vision of a future where happiness and grief can coexist, where loss does not mean the end of love, where life can still hold meaning, purpose, and joy.

167

In the aftermath of my son's death, nurturing hope for the future felt like an immense task. But each day, I discovered little pockets of hope in unexpected places. In the smile of my youngest, in the comfort of a well-read book, in the shared silence between old friends, in the tranquil solitude of my garden, in the ritual of making morning coffee, even in the process of penning down my thoughts for this book.

These were not monumental shifts, but small, gentle nudges towards acceptance, towards healing, towards a future. Each instance was a step forward, a proof that life could still hold moments of peace, joy, and yes, hope. As I nurtured these flickers, they gradually illuminated my path, leading me to a new version of life, one that held both my love for my son and my hope for the future.

Nurturing hope for the future is not about forgetting or replacing what we've lost. It's about holding our loved ones in our hearts as we forge ahead. It's about honoring our past and our grief while making room for healing, growth, and new experiences. It's about finding a delicate balance between remembering and moving on, between grieving and living.

In the face of loss, hope is our beacon, guiding us towards a future that, while different from what we had planned, can still be meaningful, fulfilling, and filled with love. As this grief journey continues, I invite you to nurture your own spark of hope. Hold it gently, protect it, let it grow. And remember, it's okay if your hope wavers or dims at times. It's part of the process. Just keep going, keep growing, and keep hoping. For as long as we have hope, we carry the promise of a new dawn within us.

Conclusion: My Final Reflection

As our journey through this book comes to a close, I hope it has provided a measure of comfort, understanding, and companionship. I hope it has shown you that grief, though a lonely road, does not have to be a solitary journey. That it is possible to find connection, support, and shared understanding even amidst profound loss. That we can build a future that honors our past, embraces our present, and nurtures hope for tomorrow.

In our shared narratives of loss, grief, resilience, and hope, we find a collective strength that buoys us through the darkest of times. In our stories, our tears, our laughter, our memories, and our dreams, we find a sense of shared humanity, a validation of our feelings, and a beacon of hope. We learn that we are not alone. That our grief is a testament to our love. That even in the face of great loss, it is possible to create a life filled with meaning, purpose, and joy.

Healing, dear reader is not about arriving at a place where the pain of loss no longer exists. It's about learning to live with that pain, to carry it alongside our love, our memories, and our resilience. It's about embracing the complex tapestry of our emotions—our sorrow, our longing, our gratitude, our joy, our hope—and acknowledging that they can coexist, that they make us who we are.

The path to healing is unique for each of us, as unique as our relationships, our losses, and our love. Your path may not look like mine, and that's okay. Remember, there's no 'right' way to grieve, no 'right' way to heal. Your grief journey is yours, and yours alone. Honor it. Respect it. Walk it at your own pace. And know that along the way, you will find strength you never knew you had, discover resilience you never thought possible, and nurture hope in places you least expected.

As I pen these final words, I am reminded of a quote by poet Rainer Maria Rilke: "Let everything happen to you: beauty and terror. Just keep going. No feeling is final." In our grief, in our healing, and in our ongoing journeys, may we embrace these words. May we let ourselves feel deeply, live fully, grieve wholly, and heal gradually. May we remember that no feeling is final, that there is always a potential for growth, for change, for hope. And most importantly, may we remember to just keep going.

Thank you for joining me on this journey, for allowing me to share my story, and for being brave enough to confront your own. As we close this chapter, I extend my heartfelt wish for your healing journey: May you find peace in your grief, strength in your sorrow, resilience in your pain, and hope in your tomorrow.

Epilogue

As we turn the final pages of this book, it's essential to remember that the journey we've walked through these chapters doesn't end here. Grief is a lifelong companion, changing shape and form as we evolve and learn to live with our loss. This journey is not a destination, but a path that we must tread, one step at a time, with courage, resilience, and most importantly, hope.

In the wake of my son's passing, I sought solace in myriad ways: counseling, support groups, spiritual practices, and creative expression, among others. I've found great strength in these traditional methods of coping with grief, but also in the unexpected places.

In the course of my grief journey, I discovered a new technology that offered me a profound source of comfort and healing. It provided an unexpected beacon of light in my darkest times, illuminating the path towards healing and acceptance. The transformative potential of this technology inspired me to delve deeper into its mechanisms and benefits, enriching my understanding of grief and loss, and offering unique perspectives on healing the broken heart.

I am eager to share this innovative technology with you, fellow companions on this grief journey, and anyone willing to explore new avenues of healing and coping with loss. Perhaps, like me, you may find that it helps to fill some of the voids, to ease some of the pain, to bring back some of the color into a world that may seem painfully monochromatic in the aftermath of such a loss.

This technology isn't a magic wand that will make grief disappear, but a tool that could potentially provide new strategies for coping and healing. It has helped me, and I believe it may offer solace to others navigating their way through grief.

If you are interested in knowing more about this new technology, feel free to reach out to me at dee.walterspublishing@gmail.com. Sharing and connecting with others who have walked this path has been a great source of strength for me, and I hope it will be for you, too.

As you close this book and resume your journey, remember that grief is not a linear process, and there is no right or wrong way to grieve. Remember, too, that love is everlasting. Though our children may not be with us physically, they live on in our hearts, our memories, and in the love, we shared with them.

In conclusion, I leave you with a promise and an invitation. The promise is that you are not alone. You are part of a community of bereaved parents who understand your pain and share your sorrow. The invitation is to reach out, share, and connect. Together, we can navigate the winding path of grief towards healing, acceptance, and ultimately, a renewed sense of purpose and hope.

Stay strong, for you are stronger than you realize. Carry your love and your memories as a lantern to guide you through the darkest nights. And know that while the path may be long and winding, it is not insurmountable. The sun still rises, even after the darkest night.

In love, strength, and hope,

Dee Walters.

www.ingramcontent.com/pod-product-compliance
Lightning Source LLC
Chambersburg PA
CBHW021637120626
46545CB00002B/579